D1030733

The Cast Iron Way to Cook

LE CREUSET
LE CREUSET

The Cast Iron Way to Cook

First Published in 2012

ISBN 978-0-9550060-5-0

Le Creuset of America, Inc.
114 Bob Gifford Boulevard
Early Branch
SC29916
USA

contents

Introduction

A history of delicious meals

For thousands of years, cast iron has been one of the most popular and effective materials for producing cookware, from Roman society through 18th-century Europe to the present. Durable and efficient, its strength and performance make it a reliable mainstay in home kitchens and restaurants today—and for nearly a century, the artisans of Le Creuset have been crafting our premium enameled cast iron cookware by hand in the French village of Fresnoy-le-Grand.

Not much has changed since 1925: each piece of our enameled cast iron is still individually cast in sand molds, then hand-inspected by 15 skilled craftsmen—ensuring that every finished piece is worthy of the Le Creuset name and the passionate chefs and food lovers around the world who prepare and serve their favorite meals with our cookware.

Today, Le Creuset is the leader in brilliantly colorful, high-performance enameled cast iron cookware that's easy to use, easy to clean and easy to care for. Throughout this book, you'll discover just how versatile cast iron can be—and how Le Creuset's timeless style, superior quality and legendary performance are still the trusted choice of those who truly love to cook.

Trusted and treasured:
Le Creuset's classic enameled cast iron

Perfected design.
Superior artisan quality.

As any artisan will tell you, there is a "right tool for the job" which will not only make the task easier, but improve the results as well. That's why Le Creuset draws from deep roots and traditional craftsmanship to produce the widest, most versatile range of specialized shapes available—so home cooks and professional chefs alike can bring delicious, succulent meals to the table.

Only Le Creuset has nearly a century of expertise designing premium enameled cast iron cookware. From ergonomic accessory handles to tight-fitting lids that provide superior heat and moisture retention and distribution, our commitment to design continues to set our cookware apart—and the passion of our artisans remains unmatched.

Unrivaled colors.
Unparalleled performance.

Since the introduction of our Volcanic Flame enameled cast iron more than 85 years ago, Le Creuset has been a leader in bold, rich color—and an innovator in the latest, most sought-after hues. Today, Le Creuset's range of signature shades continues to evolve—building on the best of the past and proving that true classics never go out of style.

Our generations of expertise in enameling and color have also enabled us to create perfectly color-matched products across our entire range, perfectly complementing our classic enameled cast iron. But it's not just our array of colors that is all-encompassing. Le Creuset enameled cast iron cookware can be used on all heat sources, including gas, electric solid plate or radiant ring, vitro-ceramic, induction, ovens fired by gas, oil, coal, or wood, and even the grill.

Easy to use. Easy to love.

Our enameled cast iron cookware is made to be enjoyed for generations, and it all starts with Le Creuset's unique interior enamels. Perfected for precise cooking and simple cleanup, our smooth, glass-like sand-colored interior is found on French Ovens, Braisers, Sauce Pans, Soup Pots, Roasters, and Au Gratins. Resistant to odor and flavor absorption, this unique protective enamel is the optimal surface for a variety of cooking techniques, and provides a light background for easily checking the doneness of food as it cooks. This is the best choice for slow cooking, braising, preparing soups and stews, and can also be used for roasting and shallow and deep frying.

Alternately, our assortment of skillets, woks, and tagines features a satin black interior enamel for high-temperature cooking. Although this special finish may make the piece appear as "raw" cast iron, it is in fact a hard-wearing enamel that does not require the traditional seasoning or maintenance of raw cast iron. As the surface's natural patina builds, less oil is required and cooking performance is enhanced for techniques like grilling, searing, and pan frying.

Cooking with Le Creuset enameled cast iron

Preparing and Preheating

When you're ready to begin cooking with your Le Creuset enameled cast iron cookware, remove any labels and stickers from the side and base, then wash and dry thoroughly.

Preheating is always a good idea with cast iron, so plan to heat your cookware on low heat for several minutes before adding ingredients. When using a pan with a black enamel interior, always test if the pan is sufficiently heated before adding oil and cooking. Simply sprinkle some water on the surface with your fingers—if the droplets pop and sizzle, then the pan is ready to use. If you're using a piece with a sand-colored enamel interior, the entire cooking surface should be covered with your choice of oil or fat for frying, or with liquid if your dish requires moisture.

Cooking on the Stove

Preparing delicious meals with Le Creuset enameled cast iron is simple, effective and fun—and this versatile material works perfectly on all stove types including glass induction cooktops. The superb heat conduction properties of the cookware make high heat settings unnecessary, as low to medium heat settings are ideal for thoroughly cooking food.

Cooking with too much heat can cause foods to stick or brown too quickly, so it is vital to avoid overheating when using cast iron on the stovetop. Low to medium heats will always provide the best results, even if you are frying or searing. Also, try to avoid adding cool liquids to a hot pan during cooking, as this sudden temperature shift could cause the enamel to crack.

When it's time to stir ingredients or flip a cut of meat or fish during cooking, it is recommended that you use silicone, plastic, or wooden utensils. While it is safe to use metal utensils with cast iron, this can gradually cause damage to the interior enamel finish over time.

Cooking in the Oven

All Le Creuset enameled cast iron is oven safe, with the classic black phenolic knobs safe up to 375°F, Signature Range composite knobs safe up to 500°F and Stainless Steel knobs safe at any normal oven temperature.

When cooking in the oven with cast iron, always use the lowest temperature possible for the recipe. Once the cookware is hot, its excellent heat retention keeps food at the optimal temperature during cooking, making higher settings unnecessary.

Cooking Outdoors

Le Creuset enameled cast iron is versatile enough for use over an open flame when cooking outdoors. Whether preparing meals on the grill or over a campfire, our durable cast iron can withstand outdoor cooking while still yielding delicious results.

Oven to Table

Le Creuset enameled cast iron's exceptional heat retention not only ensures even cooking, it also allows the cookware to double as beautifully effective serving dishes. From the oven to the stovetop to the table, Le Creuset has perfected our range of enameled cast iron cookware for both cooking and serving—

keeping hot foods warm and cold foods chilled during meals.

Cleaning and Maintenance

When cleaning Le Creuset enameled cast iron, allow it to cool before filling it with water. Filling hot cookware with cold water may damage the enamel. The cookware can usually be cleaned easily in warm soapy water with a non-abrasive sponge or brush. Dried or burnt-on food can be removed with a short soaking for 15–20 minutes.

To keep your cookware looking new, a special cast iron cleaner is available from Le Creuset. This exclusive cleaning solution removes burnt-on deposits and stains while keeping the enamel looking new inside and out.

For more thorough cleaning, Le Creuset enameled cast iron may be washed in a dishwasher if needed, but constant washing may lead to dulling of the enamel. However, this will not affect the performance of the cookware.

Lifetime Warranty

Le Creuset offers a limited lifetime warranty on its cast iron cookware against defects in manufacturing that appear during normal household use.

French Ovens

Background

Handcrafted one at a time inside our Fresnoy-le-Grand foundry for nearly a century, Le Creuset Round and Oval French Ovens have been a fixture in kitchens around the world for generations. Their enduring quality, wide-ranging versatility and stylish colors have made them indispensable in the kitchen and cherished around the table.

Cooking with French Ovens

With even heat retention, superior heat distribution and tight-fitting lids that lock in moisture and flavor, Le Creuset French Ovens are ideal for soups, stews, one-pot meals and even roasting meat. From the stovetop to the oven to the table, these workhorses of the kitchen combine the convenience of one-pot cooking with the performance of Le Creuset's high-quality, easy-to-clean interior enamel.

The True Benefit of Le Creuset

With a full assortment of capacities (from the compact 1 quart to the family-sized 13¼ quart), Le Creuset Round French Ovens offer the slow-cooking benefits of enameled cast iron on the stovetop and true kitchen-to-table capability—whether cooking for two on a busy weeknight or preparing a delicious holiday feast for ten. Our selection of Oval French Ovens provides the same slow-cooking performance with a practical oval shape designed to accommodate larger poultry, leg of lamb and longer cuts of meat—all while maximizing side-by-side space on the stovetop.

Cooking Tips

• Choosing the right size French Oven is key when preparing your recipe. A good rule of thumb when entertaining multiple guests is 1 quart of capacity for each person—therefore a 4½ or 5½ quart pot is ideal for 4–5 guests at your table.

• *A Fact About Cast Iron*
French Ovens are also commonly called casseroles or Dutch Ovens. The term "Dutch Oven" was widely adopted after the Dutch became famous for producing and exporting cookware in the 1700s.

Chicken Barley Broth Soup

SERVES: 6–8
PREPARATION TIME: 15 minutes
COOKING TIME: 2 hours
COOK IN: a 4½ quart round French oven

INGREDIENTS
1 tablespoon butter
2 onions, chopped
2 garlic cloves, minced
2 medium carrots, finely diced
7oz mushrooms, finely chopped
2 celery sticks, finely diced
1 cup pearl barley
1 teaspoon dried thyme
1 teaspoon dried sage
1 teaspoon black pepper
8 cups hot light chicken stock
8oz cooked chicken, finely shredded
4oz young greens, finely shredded
salt
warm crusty bread, to serve

The heritage of a true barley broth soup lies in Scotland where it is more commonly known as Scotch broth. This was a hearty soup made each day throughout the cold winter months to provide a warming meal. The basic ingredients varied greatly according to taste and availability, but would usually contain meat and root vegetables. Stock and pulses—and, occasionally, shredded greens or cabbage—would be added towards the end of cooking. Barley is one of the oldest cultivated cereal grains and was always included for its excellent thickening properties, as well as to give the soup a creamy texture.

1. Melt the butter in the French oven over a medium heat on top of the stove. Add the onions and garlic, and sauté for 4–5 minutes until softened, but not browned.

2. Add the diced vegetables, pearl barley, herbs, pepper, and hot stock. Once simmering, stir well, put on the lid, and cook over a low heat for 1½ hours.

3. Add the chicken and greens, stir, and continue cooking with the lid on for 15–20 minutes.

4. Season to taste with some salt and serve with the warm crusty bread.

COOKING TIPS

The recipe can also be made in a 5 quart oval French oven.

Make the most of any leftovers from a roast chicken by removing the meat and making stock from the bones. You can freeze the meat and the stock, and use them both later in this recipe.

If you are using a stock cube or liquid concentrated stock, make up to half the recommended strength to achieve a light stock.

Moules Marinières

Eat this classic French recipe as the French do by using a good-sized empty mussel shell as a pincer to pick the mussels from their shells and then mop up the delicious broth with chunks of crusty baguette. The large French oven gives the mussels plenty of room to open when cooking and also makes a stunning serving dish.

SERVES: 4
PREPARATION TIME: 15 minutes
COOKING TIME: 12–15 minutes
COOK IN: a 7¼ quart round French oven

INGREDIENTS
4½ lb fresh mussels
1½ cups dry white wine
3 echalion or banana shallots, chopped
2–3 garlic cloves, minced
½ teaspoon black pepper
½ stick unsalted butter
a good handful of chopped fresh parsley, to serve
lemon wedges and crusty French baguette, to serve

1. Wash and clean the mussels of any grit and barnacles, and remove the beards by grasping them firmly and pulling them away.

2. Put the cleaned mussels into the French oven with the white wine, cover with the lid, and heat on top of the stove over a medium heat for 2 minutes. Reduce the heat and continue to cook for a further 4–5 minutes.

3. Once all the mussels have opened, tip them into a large colander set over a bowl to catch the cooking liquid. Discard any unopened mussels.

4. Return the retained cooking liquid to the French oven, keeping back the final drop as this will contain some grit or sand from the mussels.

5. Put the French oven back on the stove over a medium heat and add the shallots, garlic, and pepper. Bring to a boil and simmer for a couple of minutes to reduce the cooking liquor by about a quarter. Taste the liquor because it can become salty if over-reduced.

6. Whisk in the butter, return the cooked mussels to the French oven, and heat through until piping hot.

7. Serve immediately from the pot with lemon wedges and the fresh parsley sprinkled over the top accompanied by plenty of crusty French baguette.

COOKING TIPS

Live mussels should smell fresh like the sea and be tightly shut. Tap widely opened shells and discard them if they stay open, along with any damaged ones, as they may be dead.

Echalion shallots are a cross between an onion and a shallot. They are sweet, juicy, and easy to peel. You can use standard shallots instead, but increase the quantity to 5.

LE CREUSET

Bouillabaisse

SERVES: 4
PREPARATION TIME: 40 minutes
COOKING TIME: about 35 minutes
COOK IN: a 5½ quart round French oven

INGREDIENTS
½ cup dry white wine
12–16 mussels, cleaned
2⅓ cups fish stock (ideally made from fish bones)
3 tablespoons olive oil
1 large onion, chopped
4 garlic cloves, sliced
1 fennel bulb, trimmed and chopped
1lb 2oz ripe tomatoes, peeled and chopped
1 tablespoon tomato paste
a bouquet garni (made up of 2 bay leaves, 2 fresh thyme sprigs, and 2 fresh fennel sprigs)
good pinch of saffron threads
2in strip of orange peel
4 potatoes, peeled and thickly sliced
salt and freshly ground black pepper
2¼ lb mixed fish, boned, skinned, and cut into large chunks
a good handful of chopped fresh parsley, to garnish
slices of baguette, toasted and rubbed with garlic, to serve

for the rouille:
6 tablespoons mayonnaise
2 teaspoons harissa paste

An authentic bouillabaisse contains a mixture of small Mediterranean rockfish, but you can make this recipe using almost any firm-fleshed white fish and shellfish. Traditionally, whole fish (still on the bone) is included and the fish and broth served separately, but it is much easier to eat if you use boned and skinned fish. Ask your fishmonger to do the hard work for you.

1. To make the rouille, mix together the mayonnaise and harissa, and set aside.

2. To make the bouillabaisse, pour the wine into the French oven. Bring to a boil and add the mussels. Cover and cook for 4–5 minutes or until the mussels have opened. Discard any unopened mussels. Set aside the cooked mussels and strain the liquid into the stock. Wash and dry the French oven.

3. Heat the olive oil in the French oven. Add the onion, garlic, and fennel, and cook for 10 minutes until soft but not colored. Add the tomatoes, tomato paste, bouquet garni, saffron, and orange peel, and stir for 1 minute.

4. Add the stock and potatoes, and season with salt and pepper. Bring to a boil, cover, and simmer for 15–20 minutes until the potatoes are quite soft.

5. Add the fish in order, starting with dense fish such as monkfish that take the longest to cook. Cook the fish for about 5 minutes until just cooked.

6. Place the mussels on top of the soup, cover, and cook for 2 minutes until piping hot.

7. Scatter with the chopped parsley and serve with the rouille and toasted bread.

COOKING TIP

Suitable fish for a bouillabaisse include red mullet, gurnard, halibut, monkfish, hake, and John Dory and any shellfish such as crab, squid, or shrimp.

Classic Pot Roast

Slow cooking a joint of meat in an oval casserole ensures that the meat will be meltingly tender and moist. This is a one-pot dish in which the vegetables and meat cook together and makes a warming and substantial supper on a cold winter's night.

SERVES: 6
PREPARATION TIME: 20 minutes
COOKING TIME: 2 hours 45 minutes
COOK IN: a 5 quart oval French oven

INGREDIENTS
1 tablespoon oil
1lb shallots
3lb 5oz boneless chuck roast joint
salt and freshly ground black pepper
1 cup red wine
1 cup beef stock
3 whole garlic cloves, peeled
1 bay leaf
1 fresh thyme sprig
1lb chantenay or baby carrots, trimmed
2lb new potatoes, peeled

1. Preheat the oven to 350°F. Heat the oil in the French oven. Add the shallots and cook, turning from time to time, until golden. Remove and set aside.

2. Season the meat with salt and pepper, place in the French oven, and cook for 5 minutes, turning to brown on all sides. Add the wine, stock, garlic, bay leaf, and thyme, and bring to a simmer. Place the lid on the French oven and cook in the oven for 1½ hours or until the meat is almost tender.

3. Add the carrots, potatoes, and browned shallots to the French oven, replace the lid, and cook for a further hour until the meat is very tender and the vegetables are cooked. Serve the meat with the vegetables and cooking liquid.

COOKING TIP

Vary the vegetables used in the pot roast according to taste and what is in season. Baby turnips, parsnips, celery, and leeks, for example, all make good additions.

LE CREUSET

Duck Cassoulet

Cassoulet is a hearty bean-based dish that originates from the south of France. There are numerous local variations, but the main ingredients usually consist of beans, pork, and sausage.

SERVES: 6
PREPARATION TIME: 45 minutes, plus overnight soaking of the beans
COOKING TIME: 3 hours 45 minutes
COOK IN: a 4½ quart round French oven

INGREDIENTS

4 confit duck legs, plus 2 tablespoons of the confit fat
1lb 2oz boned pork shoulder or belly pork, cut into 2in pieces
6 Toulouse or garlic-flavored sausages
2 onions, sliced
4 garlic cloves, sliced
3 large tomatoes, peeled and chopped
2 bay leaves
salt and freshly ground black pepper
1 tablespoon tomato paste
2 cups fresh breadcrumbs

for the beans:

1lb 2oz dried white haricot beans
2 cloves
1 onion, peeled
9oz unsmoked bacon (in one piece with the fat)
1 carrot, scrubbed and halved
3 garlic cloves
1 teaspoon black peppercorns
2 bay leaves

1. Place the beans in a bowl and cover with cold water so that it comes 1½ in above the beans. Leave to soak overnight.

2. Drain the beans and place in the French oven. Stick the cloves into the onion and add it to the beans along with the bacon, carrot, garlic, peppercorns, and bay leaves. Cover with cold water and bring to a boil. Skim the surface, cover, and simmer for 1 hour or until the beans are tender. Drain the beans, reserving the cooking liquid and discarding the bacon, onion, and carrot. Wash and dry the French oven.

3. Heat the duck fat in the French oven, add the pork, and cook until browned. Set aside on a plate. Add the sausages and cook until browned. Cut them in half and set aside with the pork. Cook the onions and garlic in the duck fat until soft, and add the tomatoes and bay leaves. Return the pork and sausage to the pan. Season the bean-cooking liquid with salt and pepper, stir in the tomato paste, and pour over the meat. Bring to a simmer, cover, and cook for 45 minutes.

4. Preheat the oven to 325°F. Remove the pork and sausages from the French oven with a slotted spoon and place in a bowl. Pour the liquid into a jug. Place a third of the beans in the bottom of the French oven with 2 pieces of duck. Cover with half the pork and sausages. Top with a third more beans and then a final layer of pork and sausages followed by the remaining beans and duck.

5. Pour the liquid into the French oven. It should come just up to the top of the beans. Add a little water, if necessary. Sprinkle half the breadcrumbs over the surface and cook in the oven for 1 hour.

6. Push the layer of breadcrumbs into the French oven and sprinkle the remaining breadcrumbs on top. Cook in the oven for a further 30 minutes until golden on top.

COOKING TIP

Duck confit can be bought ready prepared in jars or cans. Alternatively, you can make it at home by slow cooking duck legs in goose fat.

Tarragon Roasted Chicken

You might never have considered the possibility of using a covered French oven as a roasting pan, but it works exceptionally well, producing a moist succulent bird with a crisp golden skin. While the chicken is resting before being carved, the bottom of the French oven can be used on the stove to make a delicious, tarragon-flavored cream sauce.

SERVES: 6–8
PREPARATION TIME: 5 minutes
COOKING TIME: 2–2½ hours
COOK IN: a 5 quart oval French oven

INGREDIENTS

- 1–2 tablespoons softened butter, for greasing
- 4½ lb roasting chicken
- 5–6 fresh tarragon sprigs
- 1 lemon, halved
- 2 garlic cloves, peeled
- salt and freshly ground black pepper

for the sauce:

- 2 cups hot chicken stock
- ½ cup heavy cream
- 5–6 fresh tarragon sprigs, finely chopped
- 2 teaspoons cornstarch

1. Preheat the oven to 350°F. Lightly grease the inside of the French oven using a little of the butter. Wash and dry the chicken. Place the tarragon sprigs under the skin of the breast meat. Place the lemon halves and garlic cloves into the bird's cavity. Truss the chicken into shape and grease lightly all over with the remaining butter. Finally, rub a little salt and pepper into the skin and place the chicken, breast side facing up, in the French oven.

2. Cover with the lid and put in the heated oven to roast for 2–2½ hours. The chicken is cooked when the juices run clear, not pink, when the thigh is pierced with a skewer, or an instant-read thermometer measures 180°F.

3. Lift out the chicken, and cover with aluminum foil and a clean dish-towel. Leave to rest for 10–15 minutes while you make the sauce.

4. To make the sauce, pour away any excess fat from the French oven and discard. Add the hot stock to the French oven, place over a medium heat on the stove, and bring to a boil. Stir to remove any residues from the bottom, which can be incorporated into the sauce. Once the liquid is boiling, stir in the cream blended with the tarragon and cornstarch. Reduce the heat and simmer for 2–3 minutes, stirring.

5. Taste and adjust the seasoning of the sauce before serving with the carved chicken.

COOKING TIPS

The recipe can also be made in a 5½ quart round French oven.

This roasting method also works well with pork and beef. Use the same oven temperature as above and check the meat is done using a meat thermometer.

Beef Chili

SERVES: 8
PREPARATION TIME: 10 minutes
COOKING TIME: 2 hours
COOK IN: a 5 quart oval French oven

INGREDIENTS

2 teaspoons olive oil
2 onions, chopped
3 garlic cloves, finely minced
1½ lb lean ground beef
1 teaspoon chili powder (see Cooking Tips)
1 tablespoon paprika
1 tablespoon ground cumin
2 teaspoons ground dried coriander
1 teaspoon black pepper
3 tablespoons tomato paste
14oz can chopped tomatoes, plus the juice
2 cups beef stock
2 x 14oz cans kidney beans, drained and rinsed
1 green bell pepper, diced
1 red bell pepper, diced
2oz bitter sweet chocolate (minimum 70% cocoa solids), broken into small pieces
2–3 teaspoons cornstarch mixed with a little water to make a paste
salt and freshly ground black pepper
4 tablespoons chopped fresh cilantro
½ cup sour cream, to serve
2 cups grated Cheddar cheese, to serve

This rich and aromatic chili is finished with a swirl of cool sour cream and a sprinkling of grated cheese. It is delicious served with a side dish of corn bread or a crisp green salad.

1. Heat the olive oil in the French oven over a medium heat on top of the stove.
2. Add the onions and garlic, and cook for 2–3 minutes until softened. Stir in the ground beef and sear until lightly browned.
3. Stir in the chili powder, paprika, cumin, coriander, and black pepper. Continue to cook for a further few minutes.
4. Add the tomato paste, canned tomatoes, and beef stock. Bring the contents to a simmer, stir well, and put on the lid. Cook over a low heat for 1 hour.
5. Stir in the kidney beans and bell peppers, replace the lid, and continue cooking for a further 45–50 minutes until the meat is very tender.
6. Stir in the chocolate along with enough of the cornstarch and water mixture to thicken slightly. Season to taste with salt and pepper.
7. Add the fresh cilantro.
8. Serve in the French oven with bowls of sour cream and grated cheese for diners to add at the table.

COOKING TIPS

The recipe can also be made in a 5½ quart round French oven.

A standard-strength chili powder has been used in this recipe. Chili powders vary greatly in heat strength and flavor. Mild chili powders are more aromatic than hot (often containing other spices), while hot chili powders can be extremely hot.

This recipe can be made the day before, which can often improve the flavors. Cook to the end of Step 6. Cool and chill. Reheat until piping hot and continue the recipe from Step 7.

Onion, Greens, and Gruyère Panade

A panade is essentially a French savory bread pudding made from leftovers or store cupboard ingredients. There are no strict rules for the ingredients. The main components are usually day-old bread (sour dough is best if you have it), onions, greens, and cheese. Greens can be young collard greens, chard, or mature spinach, and the Gruyère can be replaced with any other similar good-flavored cheese.

SERVES: 6 as an accompaniment
PREPARATION TIME: 10 minutes, plus 10 minutes resting time
COOKING TIME: approximately 2 hours
COOK IN: a 3½ quart round French oven

INGREDIENTS

for the caramelized onions:

½ stick unsalted butter
6 medium onions, sliced
1 teaspoon sugar
a pinch of salt

for the greens:

10oz young greens, chard, or mature spinach, washed and de-stemmed

for the panade:

9oz day-old rustic bread, cut roughly into small chunks
2 cups grated Gruyère cheese
1 teaspoon black pepper
3 cups hot light vegetable stock
½ stick butter, for the top

1. To make the caramelized onions, melt the butter in a large skillet over a low to medium heat. Add the onions, sugar, and salt, reduce the heat to low, and cook slowly for about 45–50 minutes, stirring frequently until the onions are caramelized and a deep golden brown.

2. Preheat the oven to 325°F. Roughly shred the greens and lightly steam them for 2–3 minutes.

3. To make the panade, place one-third of the caramelized onions in the base of the French oven, and then layer on top one-third of the bread, one-third of the greens, and one-third of the cheese.

4. Sprinkle with a little black pepper and pour over one cup of the hot stock.

5. Repeat the layering sequence twice more. Cover with a disk of parchment paper and rest the panade for 10 minutes before baking to allow the stock to soak in.

6. Put on the lid and bake in the oven for 50 minutes to 1 hour.

7. Remove the lid and parchment paper, and dot the top with the butter. Increase the oven temperature to 375°F, return to the oven, and bake uncovered for a further 15–20 minutes until golden and crisp on top.

COOKING TIPS

Adding a little sugar when caramelizing the onions helps to deepen the flavor and speed up the cooking process.

If you are using a stock cube or liquid concentrated stock, make up to half the recommended strength to achieve a lighter stock.

Braised Rack of Lamb

Cooking a rack of lamb in a covered French oven ensures that the meat will be tender and juicy. Cooking the lamb with garlic and rosemary is a classic method of flavoring the meat.

SERVES: 4
PREPARATION TIME: 15 minutes
COOKING TIME: 50 minutes
COOK IN: a 3½ quart oval French oven

INGREDIENTS

- 2 racks of lamb, each consisting of 8 chops (French trimmed)
- 2 garlic cloves, thinly sliced
- several fresh rosemary sprigs
- salt and freshly ground black pepper
- 1 tablespoon olive oil
- 1 onion, chopped
- ½ cup red wine
- 2 cups lamb stock
- 1 teaspoon Dijon mustard
- 1 tablespoon balsamic vinegar
- 1 teaspoon cornstarch

1. Preheat the oven to 400°F. Cut a few little slits in the flesh of the lamb and insert the slivers of garlic and small pieces of rosemary. Season the lamb with the salt and pepper.

2. Heat the olive oil in the French oven on top of the stove and brown the racks of lamb on both sides. Remove and interweave the bones of the lamb as if you were preparing a guard of honor.

3. Scatter the chopped onion over the base of the French oven. Add the wine and stock, and bring to a boil. Place the lamb in the French oven, cover with the lid, and cook in the oven for 30–40 minutes, depending on how well done you would like the lamb. Remove the lamb, cover with aluminum foil, and allow to rest.

4. Meanwhile, place the French oven on the stove and bring to a boil. Simmer briskly for 5 minutes until slightly reduced. Stir in the mustard and balsamic vinegar.

5. Mix the cornstarch with a little cold water and stir into the sauce. Simmer for a minute or two until thickened. Strain the sauce into a bowl.

6. Carve the lamb into individual chops and serve with the sauce.

COOKING TIP

Ask your butcher for some lamb bones in order to prepare a fresh lamb stock.

Garlic Greens

Cooking leafy green vegetables in a steamer helps them to keep their bright colour as well as retain nutrients. These delicious greens make a wonderful accompaniment to any roasted meats or a rich casserole.

SERVES: 4
PREPARATION TIME: 10 minutes,
COOKING TIME: 6–7 minutes
COOK IN: a 3½ quart round French oven with a steamer insert

INGREDIENTS
1lb mixed leafy green vegetables (such as kale, Swiss chard, cabbage, and collard greens)
2 tablespoons olive oil
3 garlic cloves, thinly sliced
a pinch of dried chili flakes
juice of ½ lemon
salt and freshly ground black pepper

1. Wash the greens and drain thoroughly. Remove any tough stalks and shred the leaves.

2. Fill a French oven one-third full with water and bring to a boil. Place the greens in the steamer and set it on top of the French oven. Cover with the lid and steam for 4–5 minutes until the vegetables are just tender.

3. Remove the steamer, and wash and dry the French oven.

4. Heat the olive oil in the French oven. Add the garlic and the chili flakes, and cook gently for 2 minutes until the garlic is soft but not brown. Add the leaves and stir to coat in the oil.

5. Squeeze over the lemon juice and season with salt and pepper before serving.

COOKING TIP

Although the recipe suggests using a selection of different greens in order to add a variety of color, flavor, and texture to the dish, it will work just as well if you only include one type of leafy green vegetable.

Vegetable Rice

Vegetable rice dishes are highly versatile and can be served either hot or cold. The heat-retaining qualities of cast iron are so effective that the French oven can be removed from the heat as soon as it is hot and the rice will finish cooking with no additional bottom heat. Serve as an accompaniment to poultry or meat dishes.

SERVES: 6
PREPARATION TIME: 10 minutes
COOKING TIME: 25–30 minutes, including standing time
COOK IN: a 3½ quart round French oven

INGREDIENTS

2 tablespoons olive oil
1 red onion, finely chopped
½ yellow bell pepper, deseeded and chopped
½ red bell pepper, deseeded and chopped
1 cup button mushrooms, finely sliced
1¾ cups instant long grain rice
3 cups hot vegetable stock
1 cup frozen peas, thawed
1 tablespoon chopped fresh parsley
a pinch of salt
½ teaspoon black pepper

1. Heat the oil in the French oven over a medium heat on top of the stove. Add the onion, peppers, and mushrooms, and fry gently without coloring for 2–3 minutes.

2. Stir in the rice and, once the oil has been absorbed, add the remaining ingredients. Stir well, and bring to a slow boil.

3. Cover with the lid and reduce the heat to low. Simmer for 2 minutes.

4. Remove the French oven from the heat and leave it to stand for 20–25 minutes. Do not remove the lid during the standing time. Stir well before serving.

COOKING TIPS

The recipe can also be made in a 3½ quart braiser.

To give the rice a rich golden color, simply add a pinch of saffron to the hot vegetable stock.

If this dish is to be served cold, make sure you cool it as quickly as possible, transfer to the refrigerator, and use within 24 hours. Do not reheat.

Chocolate and Raspberry Cake

This rich chocolate cake has a subtle tang as a result of the raspberries. It can be eaten warm as a decadent dessert, but also slices well when served cold as a cake.

SERVES: 8–10
PREPARATION TIME: 20 minutes
COOKING TIME: 40–45 minutes
COOK IN: a 2¾ quart round French oven

INGREDIENTS

2 sticks butter, plus extra for greasing
9oz semi-sweet chocolate
1 teaspoon instant coffee
5 large eggs
scant ½ cup superfine sugar
⅔ cup all-purpose flour, sifted
6oz fresh raspberries
a little powdered sugar, for dusting

1. Preheat the oven to 325°F. Grease the inside of the French oven and line the base with a circle of parchment paper.
2. Put the chocolate, butter, coffee, and 1 tablespoon of water into a saucepan. Place over a medium heat and melt together, stirring occasionally. Cool slightly.
3. Put the eggs and sugar into a large bowl and beat until thick and pale in color. (This may take 4–5 minutes using an electric hand-mixer.)
4. Using a metal spoon, gently fold the chocolate mixture into the eggs and sugar, followed by the flour.
5. Pour the cake mixture into the French oven and sprinkle the raspberries evenly over the top.
6. Bake in the center of the oven for 40–45 minutes or until the cake is well risen and springy to the touch.
7. Leave the cake to cool for 10 minutes and then ease around the edge of the French oven with a round-bladed knife before turning the cake out onto a large serving plate.
8. When cool, remove the parchment paper and turn the cake over so that the raspberries are on the top. Dust with the powdered sugar to serve.

COOKING TIP

Frozen raspberries can be used instead. Thaw them thoroughly and drain off any excess juice.

Braisers

Background

Braising (derived from the French word for live coals or embers) uses both wet and dry heats in varied intensities to break down tough cuts of meat and tenderize fresh vegetables. Most recipes that call for braising involve first searing meat at a high temperature, then finishing covered on lower heat, creating a natural gravy.

Cooking with Braisers

The Le Creuset Braiser is designed for a variety of cooking techniques, and its low profile makes it a convenient serving solution for crowded tables and buffet-style settings.

The True Benefit of Le Creuset

From rich risottos and spicy curries to jasmine rice for a stir-fry, our enameled cast iron design is well suited for preparing a wide range of main courses and side dishes that require careful moisture control.

Cooking Tips

• In addition to braising, this classic design's flat base also allows for a variety of techniques such as poaching, searing, roasting, stir-frying, and browning.

• If food residues remain on the Braiser's sand-colored interior enamel after extended use, simply fill the pan with warm water and let it soak for 15 to 20 minutes before washing. Nylon or soft cleaning pads or brushes can be used, but in order to avoid damaging the enamel, do not use metallic pads or harsh abrasive cleaning agents.

Sausages Braised with Leeks and Sage

Tender and flavorsome sausages are cooked in an aromatic sage gravy with fresh leeks. For a special finishing touch, you could sprinkle some fried sage leaves over the sausages before serving. Accompany this dish with plenty of fluffy mashed potato and lightly steamed greens.

SERVES: 6
PREPARATION TIME: 10 minutes
COOKING TIME: 35–40 minutes
COOK IN: a 3½ quart braiser

INGREDIENTS
1–2 tablespoons olive oil
2lb good-quality chicken or pork sausages
2 tablespoons butter
14oz leeks, cleaned and sliced into ½in rounds
2 tablespoons cider vinegar
1 tablespoon wholegrain mustard
1 tablespoon dried sage
1 teaspoon black pepper
3 cups hot chicken or vegetable stock
1½ tablespoons cornstarch mixed with a little water to make a paste

to garnish (optional):
12 fresh sage leaves, plus a little butter

1. Heat the olive oil in the braiser over a low to medium heat on top of the stove. Add the sausages and brown well on all sides. Remove the sausages to a plate and set to one side. If the sausages have produced an excessive amount of oil during browning, skim it away with a spoon.

2. Melt the butter in the pan, add the sliced leeks, and stir-fry for 3–4 minutes.

3. Add the cider vinegar, followed by the mustard, dried sage, and black pepper. Pour over the hot stock and bring to a simmer.

4. Add the cornstarch mix and stir until thickened and glossy.

5. Return the browned sausages to the pan, put on the lid, and cook over a low heat for 15–20 minutes. Adjust the seasoning to taste with some salt and pepper.

6. To make the decorative sage leaves, melt the butter in a small frying pan over a low heat and cook the leaves until they are crisp, turning them once. Sprinkle over the sausages.

COOKING TIPS

The recipe can also be made in a 3½ quart round French oven.

If you are using a round French oven, you will need to separate the sausages into two batches for browning.

Chicken Pot Pie

The versatile braiser is the perfect solution for making pies. It can be used as a skillet to brown ingredients and then as a casserole to cook the pie filling when the lid is added. Finally, when you top the filling with pie crust and bake it in the oven, it becomes a pie dish.

SERVES: 4
PREPARATION TIME: 20 minutes, plus 30 minutes to 1 hour for chilling
COOKING TIME: 1 hour
COOK IN: a 1½ quart braiser

INGREDIENTS

for the pie crust:

8oz all-purpose flour, plus a little extra for dusting
½ stick shortening
½ stick butter
¼ teaspoon salt
2–3 tablespoons water, to mix
1 beaten egg, to wash

for the filling:

2 tablespoons butter
1 cup peeled and quartered shallots
10oz skinless chicken breast, diced
¾ cup hot chicken stock
1 cup chantenay or baby carrots
1 cup baby button mushrooms
½ teaspoon black pepper
½ teaspoon dried sage
½ teaspoon dried thyme
2 tablespoons cornstarch
¾ cup heavy cream
1 cup chopped green beans
1 cup frozen peas
a pinch of crushed sea salt flakes

1. To make the pie crust, put the flour, fats, and salt into a bowl. Using your fingertips or a food-processor, work the fat into the flour until it resembles breadcrumbs. Add just enough water to combine and gently work into a smooth dough. Wrap in plastic wrap and rest in a cool place for 30 minutes to 1 hour.

2. To make the filling, melt the butter in the braiser over a low to medium heat on top of the stove. Sauté the shallots in the butter for 5–6 minutes until lightly browned.

3. Add the chicken a few pieces at a time and stir-fry for 3–4 minutes. Stir in the hot stock, carrots, mushrooms, black pepper, and dried herbs. Bring to a simmer before placing on the lid, reduce the heat to low, and cook for 10 minutes.

4. Mix the cornstarch with the cream and stir a little at a time into the braiser's contents. Once the sauce has thickened, adjust the seasoning to taste. Stir in the green beans and frozen peas, remove from the heat, and leave to cool.

5. Preheat the oven to 375°F. To make the pie, roll out the pie-crust dough on a lightly floured board into a circle that is ¾in larger in diameter than the lid of the braiser. Egg wash the rim and outer top edge of the dish. Place the pie crust over the filling, overlapping the top of the dish, and gently press down around the edges to seal. Egg wash and make 4 steam holes in the top of the pie crust.

6. Sprinkle over the sea salt and bake in the upper part of the oven for 35–40 minutes until the top is golden brown.

COOKING TIPS

Pie-crust dough can be made in advance and kept for up to 3 days in the refrigerator or frozen for up to 3 months.

When making the pie-crust top, use the lid of the braiser as a guide by placing it on top of the rolled-out dough and cutting out a circle that is ¾in larger than the lid.

LE CREUSET

Spiced Meatballs with Linguini

SERVES: 6
PREPARATION TIME: 30 minutes, plus at least 1 hour chilling time
COOKING TIME: 40 minutes
COOK IN: a 3½ quart braiser

INGREDIENTS

1lb dried linguini

for the meatballs:

1lb ground lean beef
8oz ground lean pork
1 medium onion, finely chopped
2 cups fresh white breadcrumbs
½ teaspoon hot chilli powder
1 teaspoon ground allspice
2 tablespoons chopped fresh flat-leaf parsley
½ teaspoon salt
¼ teaspoon freshly ground black pepper
1 large egg, beaten
flour, for dusting
2 tablespoons olive oil, for frying

for the sauce:

2 tablespoons olive oil, if needed
1 onion, finely chopped
2 garlic cloves, crushed
1 red bell pepper, deseeded, quartered, and cut into thin slices
2lb canned plum tomatoes, chopped with their juice
2 bay leaves
2 tablespoons chopped fresh flat-leaf parsley
salt and freshly ground black pepper

This delicious recipe is ideal for cooking in a braiser because you need a wide pan to fry the meatballs, as well as a pan with a lid to cook them in. You can, however, also cook this recipe in a large frying pan with a lid.

1. Put all the meatball ingredients except the oil into a large bowl and mix thoroughly. Turn out onto a well-floured surface and divide into 24 equal pieces.

2. Using wet hands, form each piece into a ball and place on a baking sheet, spacing well apart. Cover and refrigerate for at least 1 hour before frying.

3. Heat the oil in the braiser over a medium heat on the stove. Add a few meatballs at a time and fry until they are all evenly brown, transferring them to the upturned lid as they brown.

4. To make the sauce, add a little more oil to the braiser if necessary, add the onion, garlic, and bell pepper, and fry until they begin to soften.

5. Add the tomatoes with their juice, the bay leaves, parsley, and a little salt and freshly ground black pepper.

6. Return the meatballs to the sauce, cover, and simmer for 20–30 minutes, turning the meatballs over at least once.

7. While the meatballs are cooking, cook the linguini until it is al dente and then drain well.

8. Divide the linguini between 6 serving plates and top with the meatballs and a little sauce. Remove the bay leaves before serving.

COOKING TIPS

If you make the meatballs from fresh meat, they can be frozen at the end of Step 2, so that they are ready in advance when you want to make the dish. Thaw before cooking.

This classic Italian dish deserves a wine of Italian heritage. A good-quality Chianti makes an excellent accompaniment or you could also try one of the Sangiovese-based red wines from California.

Wild Mushroom Risotto

The cost of good dried porcini or chanterelle mushrooms may appear to be high, but only a small amount is required to give this risotto a superb flavor. Unlike the majority of the recipes in the book, this one does need attention while it is cooking, but the results are well worth it.

SERVES: 4 as an appetizer or 2–3 as a main course
PREPARATION TIME: 25 minutes, plus soaking time
COOKING TIME: 40 minutes
COOK IN: a 3½ quart braiser

INGREDIENTS

1 cup loosely packed dried porcini or chanterelle mushrooms
1 tablespoon butter, softened
1 tablespoon extra-virgin olive oil
1 medium onion, finely chopped
2 garlic cloves, crushed
1¾ cups arborio rice
1¾ cups chestnut mushrooms, thinly sliced
1 cup dry white wine
5 cups hot chicken stock
1 teaspoon salt
⅛ teaspoon freshly ground black pepper
fresh chopped parsley, to garnish
1 tablespoon finely grated Parmesan cheese, to serve

1. Put the dried mushrooms into a small bowl. Cover with 1 cup of very hot water and leave to soak for at least 30 minutes. Drain and reserve the soaking liquid.

2. Melt the butter with the oil in the braiser over a medium heat on top of the stove. Add the onion and fry gently until it begins to soften. Lower the heat if the onion begins to color.

3. Add the garlic and rice, and stir until all the butter and oil are absorbed. Stir in the chestnut mushrooms and roughly chopped soaked mushrooms.

4. Move the braiser away from the heat and stir in 4 tablespoons of the mushroom-soaking liquid, taking care not to add the gritty sediment in the bottom. Add the wine and 1 cup of the hot stock with the seasonings. Return the braiser to the heat, stir well, and simmer very gently for 10–15 minutes, stirring occasionally.

5. Add another cup of the hot stock and continue simmering and stirring for a further 10–15 minutes. Repeat this process for a further 3 minutes until all the stock has been used up. After the last addition, stir frequently. The consistency should be very moist and creamy with the rice grains soft, but remaining whole.

6. Serve from the braiser sprinkled with parsley and the grated Parmesan cheese over the top.

COOKING TIPS

The recipe can also be made in a 1¾ quart skillet.

Fresh wild mushrooms can be found in some supermarkets. Use 1¾ cups of these instead of the dried version. In this case, use 1 cup of extra chicken stock to replace the mushroom-soaking liquid.

The mushrooms in this dish make it well suited to lighter-bodied red wines. A good-quality Cru Beaujolais, such as Brouilly or Fleurie, or an Italian Barbera are top choices.

Braised Fennel with White Wine and Parmesan

A braiser is ideal for cooking this Italian-style dish because it can be used on top of the stove for gently braising the fennel and then popped under the broiler to brown the Parmesan crumbs.

SERVES: 4
PREPARATION TIME: 5 minutes
COOKING TIME: 30–35 minutes
COOK IN: a 3½ quart braiser

INGREDIENTS

3 fennel bulbs
2 tablespoons butter
salt and freshly ground black pepper
½ cup dry white wine
½ cup vegetable stock
3 tablespoons grated Parmesan cheese
2 tablespoons breadcrumbs

1. Trim the fennel bulbs and discard the stems. Reserve the fronds. Trim a very slim slice from the base of each bulb, but make sure that the bulbs still hold together. Cut the bulbs into thick slices.

2. Heat the butter in the braiser. Add the fennel slices in a single layer and season with the salt and pepper. Press the slices down into the braiser. Allow to cook for 3–4 minutes until beginning to brown, and then carefully turn over the slices and brown them on the other side. (This may need to be done in two batches.)

3. Pour in the wine and allow to bubble for a minute or two before adding the stock. Bring to a boil, cover, and simmer for 20–30 minutes until the fennel is very tender. By this time most of the liquid should have been absorbed. If not, cook uncovered for a few minutes until it has reduced.

4. Preheat the broiler. Mix together the Parmesan and breadcrumbs, and scatter over the fennel. Place under the broiler and cook for 1–2 minutes until crisp and browned.

5. Chop the reserved fennel fronds and sprinkle over the top before serving.

COOKING TIP

The mild aniseed flavor of fennel goes particularly well with fish.

Roasted Brussels Sprouts with Bacon and Pecans

Even those people who think that they do not really like sprouts will be converted when they taste them cooked in this way. Roasting brings out their natural sweetness and rich nutty flavor.

SERVES: 4
PREPARATION TIME: 10 minutes
COOKING TIME: 35–40 minutes
COOK IN: a 3½ quart braiser

INGREDIENTS
1lb 5oz Brussels sprouts
2oz bacon lardons
½ cup pecans, roughly chopped
salt and freshly ground black pepper
1 tablespoon balsamic vinegar

1. Preheat the oven to 375°F. Trim the sprouts and cut them in half if they are large.
2. Heat the braiser. Add the bacon lardons and the pecans, and cook for 4 minutes or until the bacon is crisp. Remove the lardons and nuts from the braiser.
3. Add the sprouts to the braiser. Stir and then season with salt and pepper.
4. Put the braiser in the oven and roast the sprouts for 20–30 minutes, depending on their size, until they start to brown and become tender, while still retaining some "bite." Stir halfway through the cooking time.
5. Add the bacon and pecans, and return to the oven to heat through for 2–3 minutes.
6. Drizzle with the balsamic vinegar, toss, and serve.

COOKING TIP

Serve these Brussels sprouts with roast meat and poultry or grilled chops and steak.

Skillets

Background

Cast iron skillets have long been treasured kitchen staples for stovetop frying and oven baking—and our range of enameled cast iron skillets delivers that same level of reliable performance time and time again.

Cooking with Skillets

With a durable satin black interior enamel and brilliant exterior enamel, Le Creuset Skillets are protected inside and out from chipping, cracking, and excessive wear. Over time, the slightly abrasive interior develops a natural patina that should not be removed, making the pan ideal for searing and frying over low and medium heat. Cooking with too much heat can cause foods to stick or brown too quickly.

It is vital to avoid overheating when using cast iron on the stovetop—low to medium heats will always provide the best results, even if you are frying or searing. When cooking is complete, the specially designed pouring rim makes it easy to drain off excess fat or pour off deglazed sauces.

The True Benefit of Le Creuset

Le Creuset enameled cast iron Skillets come in a range of shapes and capacities, from the oversized Oval Skillet to the versatile Square Skillet Grill. And because their satin black interior does not require seasoning, they deliver perfectly prepared foods and years of reliable use.

Cooking Tips

- Comfort foods like cornbread are often prepared in a cast iron skillet lined with bacon drippings or vegetable oil—and chefs everywhere attest to the cast iron skillet's unique ability to produce the desired balance of a crispy golden crust and a soft, fluffy interior.

- A small amount of oil should cover the surface and take on a gently rippled appearance when it's hot enough to begin cooking. In order to prevent sticking, marinated meat should be patted dry before searing.

Classic Omelette with Fines Herbes

There is a great deal of controversy about what makes a perfect omelette and how it should be cooked—and all this for one of the world's simplest dishes! The real key to success is very fresh eggs (ideally at room temperature), unsalted butter, and a good heavy omelette pan or skillet at the correct temperature.

SERVES: 1
PREPARATION TIME: 2–3 minutes
COOKING TIME: 3 minutes
COOK IN: an 8in omelette pan

INGREDIENTS

2 extra large eggs
1 teaspoon snipped fresh chives
1 teaspoon chopped fresh chervil
1 teaspoon chopped fresh parsley
a little salt and freshly ground black pepper
1 tablespoon unsalted butter

1. Lightly beat the eggs, herbs, and seasonings together in a small bowl until the yolks and whites are just broken into each other. Melt the butter in the pan over a medium heat. As the butter melts, tilt the pan so that it completely covers the bottom. When the butter almost ceases to foam and is just on the point of coloring, pour in the eggs.

2. As soon as the eggs are in the pan, use the back of a fork in a circular movement to gently move the eggs from the sides to the middle of the pan. Tilt the pan so that the runny egg at the middle flows to the side. Continue to cook for about 30 seconds until the eggs are just set but still creamy on top. Turn off the heat because there will be sufficient retained heat to complete the cooking.

3. Slide a spatula under the side of the omelette nearest to the handle. Tipping the pan away from you, roll the omelette out of the pan onto a warmed serving plate. Serve immediately so that the omelette remains soft and creamy inside.

COOKING TIPS

A 1⅜ quart skillet or non-stick frying pan can also be used for this recipe.

Do not begin heating the pan on a high setting thinking that this will save time. If the pan is overheated, it will take time to cool to the correct temperature and the omelette will be over-colored and tough on the outside and undercooked on the inside. Overheating may also cause the omelette to stick to the satin black enamel surface.

Raw or undercooked egg should not be served to the very young, elderly, or anyone whose immune system is compromised. If this is the case, either cook for a minute or so longer or slide the pan under a hot broiler for a few seconds to cook the surface before rolling the omelette out of the pan.

Mediterranean Baked Fish

An iron-handle skillet is the ideal pan in which to cook this dish because it can be started off on top of the stove and then placed in the oven to finish cooking the fish.

SERVES: 4
PREPARATION TIME: 15 minutes
COOKING TIME: about 15 minutes
COOK IN: a 1¾ quart iron-handle skillet

INGREDIENTS

3 tablespoons olive oil
6 scallions, sliced
1 garlic clove, sliced
14oz tomatoes, peeled and roughly chopped
juice of ½ lemon
1 tablespoon capers
½ cup pitted black olives, roughly chopped
salt and freshly ground black pepper
1 tablespoon roughly chopped fresh basil, plus extra leaves to garnish
4 thick white fish fillets, such as seabass, tilapia, snapper, or halibut, each weighing about 5½ oz
lemon wedges, to serve

1. Preheat the oven to 350°F. Heat 2 tablespoons of the olive oil in the skillet. Add the spring onions and garlic, and cook for 1 minute.

2. Stir in the tomatoes, lemon juice, capers, and olives, and season with salt and pepper. Cook for 2 minutes until the tomatoes start to soften. Stir in the basil.

3. Place the fish on top of the sauce, season with salt and pepper, and drizzle over the remaining olive oil. Bake in the oven for 7–10 minutes until the fish is cooked and flakes when tested with a knife. Garnish with some basil leaves and serve with lemon wedges.

COOKING TIPS

The recipe can also be made in a 1 quart au gratin dish or a 2¼ quart braiser.

To peel fresh tomatoes, score the tomatoes with a sharp knife and place in a bowl. Cover the tomatoes with boiling water and leave for 2 minutes. Remove them from the water and peel the skin away with your fingertips.

Peppered Steaks with Red Wine Sauce

If you have access to two skillets, or one frying pan and a skillet, cook the steaks and sauce side by side. If not, make the sauce first, keep it hot in another pan, and then add to the steaks at the end.

SERVES: 4
PREPARATION TIME: 15 minutes
COOKING TIME: 10 minutes for the sauce and 4–6 minutes for the steaks
COOK IN: a 1¾ quart iron-handle skillet or frying pan

INGREDIENTS
4 fillet steaks, each weighing about 8oz
2 tablespoons vegetable oil
2 tablespoons black peppercorns, crushed
½ teaspoon coarse sea salt

for the wine sauce:
1 tablespoon softened butter
1 tablespoon vegetable oil
2 shallots, finely chopped
1 garlic clove, crushed
1 tablespoon all-purpose flour
1 cup red wine (such as Cabernet Sauvignon or Zinfandel)
1 teaspoon mild prepared mustard
1 teaspoon sugar
1 tablespoon tomato paste
salt and freshly ground black pepper

1. Prepare the steaks by brushing both sides with a little of the vegetable oil and then turning them in a mixture of the peppercorns and salt, pressing it well into the surface.

2. To make the wine sauce, melt the butter with the oil in the skillet or frying pan over a medium heat. Add the shallots and fry, stirring, until they begin to soften. Add the garlic and fry for a further minute.

3. Add the flour and stir until it absorbs the excess butter and oil. Gradually stir in the red wine, mustard, sugar, and tomato paste with seasoning to taste. Simmer slowly, while cooking the steaks.

4. To cook the steaks, heat the remaining vegetable oil in another pan over a medium heat. When hot, add the steaks and cook for 2–3 minutes on each side, adjusting the cooking time to suit your taste. Take care when cooking because the peppercorns will give off a pungent aroma; use an overhead extractor if possible.

5. When the steaks are cooked, pour the sauce into the pan, warm through briefly, and serve with a little of the sauce spooned around the steaks.

COOKING TIPS
The recipe can also be made in the base of a 3½ quart braiser.

Thick sliced lamb from the leg can be used instead of steak.

A full-bodied red wine is the perfect partner for the steak. A Cabernet Sauvignon or Syrah from California or Australia are top choices. A bold peppery Californian Zinfandel also works well. You may want to use the same wine for the sauce.

Rhubarb and Orange Crumble

An iron-handle skillet is not just useful for savory dishes or steaks cooked on the stove. It also makes an ideal baking pan for fruit crumbles, cobblers, or cakes. This dessert is simple to make and can be eaten hot or cold with ice cream, whipped cream, or yogurt.

SERVES: 6
PREPARATION TIME: 20 minutes
COOKING TIME: 20–25 minutes
COOK IN: a 1¾ quart iron-handle skillet

INGREDIENTS
1lb 10oz young rhubarb, leaves removed and discarded
butter, for greasing
heaping ½ cup light brown sugar
finely grated zest of 1 orange
¼ cup orange juice

for the crumble topping:
2 cups all-purpose flour, sifted
1 stick chilled butter, diced
¼ cup light brown sugar
½ cup slivered almonds

1. Preheat the oven to 350°F and lightly butter the skillet. Cut the rhubarb into ½in pieces and put them into the skillet.

2. Stir in the sugar, orange zest, and orange juice.

3. To make the crumble topping, put the flour, butter, sugar, and half the almonds into a food-processor and process until the mixture resembles fine breadcrumbs. If you do not have a food-processor, cut or rub the butter into the flour, and then add the sugar. Crush half the almonds and stir them into the flour mixture.

4. Spoon the crumble over the top of the rhubarb, pressing it down lightly. Scatter the remaining almonds evenly over the top.

5. Bake in the center of the oven for 20–25 minutes until the top is firm and pale golden brown. Serve straight from the skillet.

COOKING TIPS
The recipe can also be made in the base of a 2¼ quart braiser.

If you or your guests have a nut allergy, omit the almonds.

This recipe is also delicious if made with fresh stoned and halved apricots.

Cornbread with Cinnamon Honey Butter

Skillet-baked, southern-style cornbread has a denser texture and is less sweet than its sister variations from the northern American states. Traditionally baked in a flat pan or skillet, cornbread is the original soul food. It is generally used as an accompaniment for dipping and mopping up both savory and sweet liquids. Quick, simple, and inexpensive to prepare, it is a common addition to the table, whether for everyday meals or Thanksgiving celebrations.

SERVES: 6
PREPARATION TIME: 10–15 minutes
COOKING TIME: 32–38 minutes
COOK IN: a 1¾ quart iron-handle skillet

INGREDIENTS

1 extra large egg
2 cups buttermilk
2 cups medium stoneground yellow cornmeal
1 teaspoon baking soda
1½ teaspoons baking powder
¼ teaspoon salt
1 teaspoon sugar
3 tablespoons melted butter
2 tablespoons butter, for frying

for the sweet butter:
1 stick softened butter
⅓ cup honey
1 teaspoon ground cinnamon

1. Preheat the oven to 375°F. To make the cornbread batter, whisk the egg until frothy and add the buttermilk. Mix together all the dry ingredients and beat into the egg and milk. Finally, whisk in the melted butter.

2. Heat the 2 tablespoons of butter in the skillet on top of the stove. Once bubbling, pour in the batter mixture, cook for 2–3 minutes, and transfer to the hot oven to bake for 30–35 minutes.

3. To make the sweet butter, whip the butter and honey with the cinnamon powder until soft and fluffy.

4. Serve the warm cornbread with the sweet butter.

COOKING TIPS

The recipe can also be made in a 2 quart tatin dish.

Freeze any leftover cornbread and use as breadcrumbs to make excellent stuffings.

Cornmeal is milled from the grain of golden maize and is also known as polenta.

Crêpe Pans

Background

Whether topped with rich chocolate and powdered sugar for dessert or filled with fruit for a weekend breakfast, crêpes have become a dish internationally identified with France as a whole, although the thin pancakes originated in the region of Brittany.

Cooking with Crêpe Pans

With its flat, low-edged design and specially designed cooking surface, this French-inspired pan produces light, thin, and perfectly browned crêpes and pancakes, yet is versatile enough for preparing individual-sized pizzas and even blinis.

The True Benefit of Le Creuset

Finished in Le Creuset's bold exterior enamel and surrounded by low-profile, gently sloping sides, our Crêpe Pan makes a unique and decorative addition to any stovetop. Its flat cooking surface is ideal for spreading batter thinly and heating it evenly.

Cooking Tips

• Skim or 2% milk will make lighter crêpe batter, but whole milk makes a slightly firmer consistency that can be easier to handle during cooking.

• Cooked crêpes and pancakes can be made in advance and frozen for up to 2–3 months.

Wholewheat Blinis with Smoked Salmon and Crème Fraîche

These blinis are extremely easy to make and make versatile buffet or appetizer bases. They can be made hours, or even weeks, in advance of a party because they freeze well.

MAKES: approximately 75 x 2in blinis
PREPARATION TIME: 10 minutes for the batter, plus 1–1½ hours standing time, and 10 minutes for the topping
COOKING TIME: 30 minutes
COOK IN: a 10¾ in crêpe pan

INGREDIENTS
1 cup wholewheat flour
1 cup all-purpose flour
¼ oz envelope of active-dry yeast
1 teaspoon salt
1½ cups warmed milk
2 large eggs, beaten
2 tablespoons vegetable oil, for frying

for the topping:
1 cup crème fraîche
8oz smoked salmon, thinly sliced
fresh dill sprigs, to garnish

1. To make the blinis, put both the flours in a large bowl with the yeast and salt. Stir in the warmed milk and the beaten eggs. Cover loosely with plastic wrap and leave to stand in a warm place for 1–1½ hours until the mixture has almost doubled in volume.

2. Heat the crêpe pan over a medium heat and brush with a little oil. Drop 5 or 6 tablespoons of the batter, spaced apart, into the pan and cook until the blinis are golden brown underneath and bubbling on top. Turn them over and cook on the other side. Remove from the pan and leave to cool on a plate.

3. Lightly brush the pan with oil between batches and continue cooking the blinis until all of the batter has been used up.

4. Spoon a small amount of the crème fraîche on the top of each blini, followed by some of the smoked salmon.

5. Garnish the topped blinis with small sprigs of dill.

COOKING TIPS

The recipe can also be made in a 1¾ quart skillet or on a flat-surface grill.

To freeze the plain blinis, leave them to cool completely and then place them in plastic boxes, interleaved with wax paper. Freeze for up to 2 months. Thaw before finishing with the topping.

For a vegetarian alternative, place small pieces of roasted vegetables on top of the crème fraîche instead of the smoked salmon.

Buttermilk Pancakes with Cherries and Mascarpone

The mascarpone cheese used in this recipe makes for a lovely combination with the warm cherry topping, but ice cream is just as good. For a little luxury, you can also add two tablespoons of cherry brandy to the preserve.

MAKES: 12 x 5in pancakes
PREPARATION TIME: 15 minutes
COOKING TIME: 15 minutes
COOK IN: a 10¾ in crêpe pan

INGREDIENTS

1½ cups all-purpose flour, sifted
4 tablespoons sugar
1 teaspoon baking powder
¼ teaspoon salt
½ teaspoon baking soda
1 cup buttermilk
½ cup milk
3 tablespoons butter, melted
2 large eggs
1–2 tablespoons vegetable oil, for cooking

for the topping:

1lb jar cherry preserve
8oz mascarpone cheese

1. Sift all the dry ingredients for the pancake batter into a bowl. Make a well in the middle of the mixture.

2. Beat together all the wet ingredients except for the vegetable oil and gradually add these to the flour, beating between additions.

3. To cook the pancakes, heat the crêpe pan over a medium heat. When it is hot, brush over a thin coating of vegetable oil. Pour about ¼ cup of the batter into the pan and cook until bubbles break through the upper surface. Using a pancake turner or spatula, turn the pancake over and cook on the other side. Keep the pancakes warm on a plate loosely covered with aluminum foil while you cook the remaining batter.

4. To make the topping, warm the cherry preserve in a small pan over a low heat.

5. To serve, spoon some of the warmed cherry preserve over half a pancake and put a spoonful of the mascarpone cheese on the other half. Serve immediately.

COOKING TIPS

The recipe can also be made in a 1¾ quart skillet or in a frying pan.

These pancakes make a good basic base for any topping or filling, whether sweet or savory. (Do not add the sugar for savory pancakes, but add a few dried herbs instead.) Scrambled eggs make a particularly good savory topping.

Crêpes Suzette

Crêpes are very special, paper-thin, buttery "pancakes," and are very French. They may be sweet or savory, large or small, and can feature in almost any meal at any time of the day. Crêpes freeze well, which means that they can be made in advance.

MAKES: 12 x 8in crêpes
PREPARATION TIME: 10 minutes for the batter, plus 1 hour standing time, and 5 minutes for the sauce
COOKING TIME: 20 minutes
COOK IN: a 10¾ in crêpe pan

INGREDIENTS
1 cup all-purpose flour
¼ teaspoon salt
2 large eggs
1 cup milk
2 tablespoons butter, melted and cooled
vegetable oil, for greasing the pan

for the sauce:
½ stick butter
2oz white sugar
zest of 1 large orange
juice of 2 large oranges (approximately ¾ cup)
1 large orange, peeled with a knife and cut into 8 slices
⅓ cup Grand Marnier
2 tablespoons French brandy or Cognac

1. To make the batter, sift the flour and salt into a bowl. Make a well in the middle of the flour and add the eggs and half the milk. Whisk until smooth.

2. Whisk in the remaining milk and cooled butter. Leave the batter to stand for 1 hour before using. If the consistency thickens after standing, add 2–3 tablespoons of milk (it should be similar in consistency to unwhipped whipping cream).

3. To cook the crêpes, heat the pan over a medium heat. When hot, lightly brush the surface with a little vegetable oil and add about scant ¼ cup of batter. Swirl it around the pan and use the rateau to spread it out thinly. Cook until bubbles begin to rise through the surface. Turn the crêpe over and cook on the other side until it is a pale golden brown. Slide the crêpe onto a plate.

4. Cook the remaining crêpes, lightly brushing the pan with vegetable oil every two to three crêpes. Stack the cooked crêpes on top of each other; they will not stick together. Cover with a piece of aluminum foil to keep them warm while you make the sauce.

5. To make the sauce, heat the butter and sugar in a large deep frying pan or large shallow casserole over a low heat, stirring until the sugar has dissolved. Add the orange juice and zest, bring to a simmer, and cook for 4–5 minutes until reduced by roughly a third. Stir in the orange slices and the Grand Marnier.

6. Add one crêpe at a time to the sauce and fold in half and then in half again, pushing each folded crêpe to one side until all the crêpes are in the pan.

7. Finally, pour over the brandy or cognac, and ignite. Serve immediately from the pan.

COOKING TIPS

The recipe can also be made in a 1⅜ quart skillet or in a frying pan.

Cooked crêpes can be frozen for 2–3 months.

Grills

Background

Le Creuset enameled cast iron Grills allow for higher surface temperatures to be achieved during frying, grilling and searing. As sugars and enzymes are released during cooking, the food's exterior will caramelize, aiding in the retention of moisture and flavor and producing sear lines on grilled meats.

Cooking with Grills

These convenient cooking surfaces perform both on the stovetop and under the broiler thanks to their durable cast iron construction. It is vital to avoid overheating when using cast iron on the stovetop—low to medium heats will always provide the best results, even if you are frying or searing. When cooking is complete, the specially designed pouring rim makes it easy to drain off excess fat and oil.

The True Benefit of Le Creuset

The ribbed base of Le Creuset enameled cast iron Grill Pans produce appetizing char lines on vegetables and meats while draining away excess fat and grease for lighter, healthier cooking. Available in a wide range of exterior colors, the interior is coated with Le Creuset's protective satin black enamel to prevent damage and wear. Over time, this slightly abrasive interior develops a natural patina that is ideal for searing and frying.

Cooking Tips

• Once the cooking surface has reached its optimal temperature on a medium setting, that temperature can generally be maintained on a lower setting due to cast iron's superior heat retention properties

• To properly preheat the pan, heat on medium, then sprinkle a few drops of water on the surface to test. Once the pan has reached the optimal temperature, brush the surface lightly with oil. The best oils for greasing are vegetable or corn oils, lightly applied with a brush or kitchen paper. Once the meat is placed on the surface to cook, leave it undisturbed for a few minutes — the caramelized sear lines that appear will allow the meat to lift easily without sticking.

Steak Kebabs with Tomato Chutney

These succulent steak kebabs have the unique chargrilled flavor that cooking on a ribbed grill produces. They taste delicious served with the rich tomato chutney.

SERVES: 4
PREPARATION TIME: 20 minutes, plus 1 hour marinating time
COOKING TIME: 10 minutes, plus 15–18 minutes for the chutney
COOK IN: a 1 quart square grill plus a 1⅜ quart iron-handle skillet or a 2¼ quart braiser for the chutney

INGREDIENTS

1¼ lb sirloin or rump steak, cut into bite-size pieces
4 x 9in skewers

for the marinade:

2 tablespoons olive oil
2 garlic cloves, crushed
½ teaspoon black pepper
2 fresh rosemary sprigs, torn into pieces
1 bay leaf, torn into pieces

for the tomato chutney:

1 tablespoon olive oil
1 medium onion, finely chopped
2 garlic cloves, minced
12oz full-flavored vine tomatoes, diced
1 mild green chili, deseeded and finely diced
1 tablespoon tomato paste
3 tablespoons light brown sugar
3 tablespoons white balsamic vinegar
a little salt, to taste
1 tablespoon chopped fresh parsley

1. Mix together all the marinade ingredients, add the steak, and cover securely with plastic wrap. Shake the container well to blend the ingredients and put in the refrigerator for a minimum of 1 hour.

2. To make the chutney, heat the oil in a medium-sized shallow pan and sauté the onions for 4–5 minutes. Add the garlic and tomatoes, and cook for a further 4–5 minutes, stirring occasionally.

3. Stir in the chili, tomato paste, sugar, and vinegar, and continue to cook for 6–8 minutes, stirring occasionally until the sauce is thick and has reduced. Check the seasoning, adding a little salt to taste, and stir in the chopped parsley. Set to one side while you cook the kebabs.

4. Drain the steak of any excess marinade, thread onto the skewers, and season well with some salt. Set the grill on the stove over a low to medium heat. Test the grill for the correct heat and cook the kebabs for 2–3 minutes on each side, adjusting the cooking time to personal taste.

5. Serve the cooked kebabs with the warm chutney.

COOKING TIPS

If you are using wooden skewers, always soak them in water before using in order to prevent charring.

Allow the kebabs to become bar-marked before turning them over because this will give them that unique chargrilled taste and also prevent sticking.

Leftover chutney is excellent served with cheese and can be kept in the refrigerator for up to 3 days.

Grilled Rib-Eye Steak with Peperonata

Peperonata is a traditional Italian stew of onions, tomatoes, and bell peppers. As well as making a delicious accompaniment to grilled steaks, it can also be used as a sauce for pasta or even as a pizza topping.

SERVES: 2
PREPARATION TIME: 15 minutes
COOKING TIME: 50 minutes
COOK IN: any grill pan and a 5½ quart round French oven or a 2¼ quart braiser for cooking the peperonata

INGREDIENTS
2 rib-eye steaks
olive oil, for brushing
salt and freshly ground black pepper
1 teaspoon chopped fresh rosemary

for the peperonata:
2 tablespoons olive oil
1 onion, sliced
1 garlic clove, crushed
2 red bell peppers, destalked and deseeded
1 yellow bell pepper, destalked and deseeded
9oz ripe tomatoes, peeled and chopped
1 tablespoon red wine vinegar
1 tablespoon capers
1 teaspoon chopped fresh thyme
1 teaspoon chopped fresh oregano
salt and freshly ground black pepper
a pinch of sugar

1. To make the peperonata, heat the oil in the French oven or braiser. Add the onion and garlic, and cook gently for 5 minutes, stirring occasionally.
2. Meanwhile, slice the peppers into strips and add to the pan. Cover and cook gently for 10 minutes.
3. Add the tomatoes, vinegar, capers, thyme, and oregano, and season with the salt, pepper, and sugar. Cook uncovered, stirring frequently, for 30 minutes until thick.
4. To prepare the steaks, brush with the olive oil and then season with salt and pepper. Sprinkle over the rosemary.
5. Heat the grill. Place the steaks on the grill and cook for about 2–3 minutes on each side until cooked to your liking.
6. Serve the steaks with the peperonata.

Capellini with Grilled Shrimp, Roasted Tomato, and Ricotta Salata

Ricotta salata is a smooth, white ewes' milk cheese originating from Sicily. It is lightly salted and then pressed, dried, and aged for at least 3 months. If it is unavailable, feta cheese can be used as a substitute.

SERVES: 2–3
PREPARATION TIME: 10 minutes
COOKING TIME: 30 minutes
COOK IN: a 2½ quart roaster, any grill pan, and a 4½ quart round French oven

INGREDIENTS

14oz baby plum tomatoes
2 tablespoons olive oil
salt and freshly ground black pepper
pinch of sugar
1 garlic clove, crushed
1 tablespoon lemon juice
7oz large, raw, peeled shrimp
10½ oz dried capellini (angel hair pasta)
a few basil leaves, roughly torn
3½ oz grated ricotta salata or crumbled feta cheese

1. Preheat the oven to 350°F. Cut the tomatoes in half and place them, cut side facing upward, in the roaster. Drizzle over 1 tablespoon of the olive oil, season with salt and pepper, and a little sugar. Roast in the oven for 20 minutes.

2. In a bowl, mix together the remaining olive oil, garlic, lemon juice, and some salt and pepper. Add the shrimp and toss to coat in the marinade.

3. Heat the grill pan. Place the shrimp on the grill and cook for 2 minutes and then turn and cook the other side for 1–2 minutes until they are pink and cooked through. Remove from the grill and set aside.

4. Meanwhile, in the French oven, cook the pasta as directed on the packet.

5. When the pasta is cooked, drain and return it to the French oven. Add the roasted tomatoes and shrimp, and stir in the basil and half the cheese.

6. Serve in warmed pasta plates with the remaining cheese scattered over the top.

Lemon and Basil Grilled Swordfish with Arugula Salad

The light fresh flavors of this swordfish recipe make it perfect for a lunch party or a light supper on a hot summer's day. Serve with chunks of crusty baguette or some new potatoes.

SERVES: 4
PREPARATION TIME: 10 minutes, plus 10 minutes marinating time
COOKING TIME: 6 minutes
COOK IN: any grill pan

INGREDIENTS

4 swordfish steaks, each weighing about 6oz
5 tablespoons olive oil
juice of 1 lemon
1 garlic clove, crushed
2 tablespoons finely shredded fresh basil leaves
salt and freshly ground black pepper
lemon wedges, to serve

for the arugula salad:
4oz arugula leaves
2oz Parmesan cheese

1. Place the swordfish steaks in a shallow dish. Mix together 4 tablespoons of the olive oil with the lemon juice, garlic, and basil leaves, and pour over the fish. Turn to coat in the marinade. Cover with plastic wrap and leave to marinate for 10 minutes.

2. Heat the grill pan. Remove the fish from the marinade and pat dry with kitchen paper. Grill for 2–3 minutes on each side until just cooked through.

3. Meanwhile, place the arugula leaves in a bowl and season with salt and pepper. Add the remaining olive oil and toss together. Shave the Parmesan cheese over the top.

4. Place the swordfish steaks on heated plates and arrange a little pile of arugula salad on top of each steak. Serve with lemon wedges.

COOKING TIP

As an alternative to swordfish, any other firm fish may be used instead. Tuna steaks cook particularly well on a grill.

Flat Bread with Caramelized Onion and Goat Cheese

SERVES: 8
PREPARATION TIME: 20 minutes, plus 30–40 minutes resting time
COOKING TIME: 1¼ hours
COOK IN: any grill pan

INGREDIENTS

for the caramelized onions:

½ stick butter
5 medium onions, sliced
1 teaspoon sugar
pinch of salt

for the flat breads:

¼ oz envelope of rapid-rise dried yeast
½ teaspoon sugar
½ cup warm milk
¼ cup plain yogurt
1 tablespoon melted butter
8oz strong white flour, plus extra for dusting
½ teaspoon salt
1 tablespoon melted butter mixed with 1 tablespoon vegetable oil, to brush the dough
5½ oz goat cheese, crumbled, to serve
a few fresh herb sprigs (such as oregano, cilantro, parsley, basil, and thyme), leaves torn, to serve

These little flat breads are ideal for party snacks, appetizers, or as a light meal. They can also be served without toppings to accompany a main meal, and they work particularly well with sauce-based main courses such as tagine dishes and curries.

1. To make the caramelized onions, melt the butter in a large skillet or frying pan over a low to medium heat. Add the onions, sugar, and salt, reduce the heat to low, and cook slowly for about 45–50 minutes, stirring frequently until caramelized and a deep golden brown.

2. To make the flat breads, add the dried yeast and sugar to the warm milk, leave for 5 minutes, and then stir in the yogurt and melted butter.

3. Combine the flour and salt in a warm bowl. Make a well in the dry ingredients, pour in the liquid, and mix together to make a dough.

4. Turn the dough out onto a floured board or silicone baking sheet and knead for a few minutes until smooth. Place the dough back in the bowl, cover with a piece of oiled plastic wrap, and put in a warm place for 30–40 minutes or until the dough has risen and become soft to the touch.

5. Divide the dough into 8 pieces, roll into balls, and flatten using a floured rolling pin until about ¼ in thick.

6. Heat the grill on the stove over a low to medium heat. Test the temperature before cooking. Lightly coat each side of the dough with the melted butter and oil mixture using a silicone brush. Grill the breads for 2–3 minutes on each side until puffed up and nicely marked with bars.

7. Serve the warm flat bread with a generous topping of caramelized onions, some crumbled goat cheese, and a sprinkling of freshly torn herbs.

Fontina, Arugula and Pancetta Panini

This quick and tasty snack takes the toasted sandwich to a new level. Cooking the paninis on a grill pan and panini press gives them a delicious chargrilled flavor, as well as attractive stripe marks from the grill ridges.

SERVES: 2
PREPARATION TIME: 5 minutes
COOKING TIME: 10 minutes
COOK IN: any grill pan

INGREDIENTS
2 individual ciabatta rolls
6 slices pancetta
1oz arugula, washed and trimmed
3½ oz fontina cheese, thinly sliced or grated

1. Heat the grill. Slice the ciabatta rolls in half horizontally.
2. Place the pancetta on the grill and cook for 2 minutes on each side until brown and crisp. Remove and drain on kitchen paper.
3. Place the ciabatta rolls, cut side facing down, on the grill and press down using a panini press, fish slice, or spatula. Cook for 1 minute.
4. Arrange the arugula on the bottom half of each roll, cover with the cheese, and then place the pancetta on top. Place the other half of the roll on top.
5. Cook the rolls on the grill, pressing down firmly with a preheated panini press for 2–3 minutes. Alternatively, press down with a fish slice or spatula and cook for 2 minutes on each side until marked with bars.
6. Cut each roll in half before serving.

COOKING TIP

Taleggio cheese is a good alternative to fontina, and prosciutto could be used instead of the pancetta.

Mediterranean Vegetables with Dill and Yogurt Sauce

This recipe makes a flavorsome hot appetizer or side vegetable dish to serve with grilled or barbecued steaks, chicken, or fish. It is perfect for serving at a summer barbecue or buffet.

SERVES: 4–6
PREPARATION TIME: 10 minutes, plus 1 hour marinating time
COOKING TIME: 20 minutes
COOK IN: any grill pan and a large au gratin dish for marinating

INGREDIENTS
12oz firm eggplant
2 medium zucchini
2 yellow summer squash
2 red bell peppers
1–2 tablespoons vegetable oil, for brushing the grill

for the marinade:
½ cup olive oil
2 tablespoons white balsamic vinegar
1 teaspoon coarse sea salt
freshly ground black pepper

for the dipping sauce:
1 cup low-fat, strained plain yogurt
2–3 teaspoons chopped fresh dill
1 garlic clove, chopped
finely grated zest of 1 lemon

1. Remove the ends from the eggplant, zucchini, and yellow squash. Cut the vegetables across into slices, ½ in thick. Cut the red peppers in half, remove the green stalks and seeds, and cut into 1½ in pieces. Transfer the prepared vegetables to the large au gratin dish.

2. Mix all the marinade ingredients together and pour over the vegetables, turning them with your hands to ensure that they are evenly coated with the marinade. Leave to stand for 1 hour.

3. Meanwhile, mix together the ingredients for the sauce and leave to stand for 1 hour.

4. Drain the vegetables and pat off any excess marinade with some kitchen paper.

5. Heat the grill pan over a medium heat on the stove and brush the ribs lightly with vegetable oil when it is hot. Add the vegetables, a few at a time, and grill for 2–3 minutes on each side.

6. Transfer the vegetables to a warm serving dish and keep hot while you cook the remaining vegetables. Serve with the dipping sauce.

COOKING TIPS

If you cannot get hold of yellow summer squash, you can use yellow bell peppers instead. These should be prepared in the same way as the red bell peppers.

If left to cool completely, these vegetables can also be used in salads. They are especially good mixed with diced mozzarella cheese, cherry tomatoes, and green olives with a generous drizzle of olive oil over the top.

Grilled Peaches with Blackberry Sauce

Serving grilled summer peaches with a rich blackberry sauce gives a hint of cooler fall days to come. This simple dessert is delicious eaten warm with lots of vanilla ice cream.

SERVES: 4
PREPARATION TIME: 10 minutes
COOKING TIME: 5–7 minutes
COOK IN: any grill pan

INGREDIENTS

4 peaches
1 tablespoon soft brown sugar
1 teaspoon balsamic vinegar
4 tablespoons blackberry or mixed berry jelly
juice of ½ lemon
1 teaspoon chopped fresh mint leaves
vanilla ice cream, to serve
mint sprigs, to decorate

1. Heat the grill on the stove. Cut the peaches in half and twist to remove the stone.

2. In a small bowl, mix together the sugar and vinegar. Brush the mixture over the cut edges of the peaches.

3. Place the peaches, cut side facing down, on the grill and cook for 3–4 minutes until golden brown. Turn the peaches over and cook for a further 2–3 minutes until they are heated through.

4. Meanwhile, place the jelly, lemon juice, and mint in a small saucepan and heat until melted.

5. Place the peaches on serving plates and drizzle over generously with the blackberry sauce. Decorate with mint and serve with ice cream.

COOKING TIP

Nectarines could be used instead of peaches. Choose fruit which is ripe but firm.

Au Gratin Dishes

Background

Named for the classic French technique of topping a dish with a crust of breadcrumbs or cheese, Le Creuset enameled cast iron Gratins come in a variety of sizes, all distinguished by the shallow, elongated shape that creates a perfectly browned crust.

Cooking with Au Gratins

From desserts like cakes and pastries to side dishes like potatoes au gratin, this functional design makes a beautiful serving dish in addition to its performance in the kitchen.

The True Benefit of Le Creuset

The cast iron construction of our Gratins makes them useful for everything from deglazing to baking. And with classic details like scalloped side handles on the Heritage Collection Oval Au Gratin, each piece pays homage to the original generation of Le Creuset style.

Cooking Tips

• When making a gratin recipe, fill the dish almost to the brim so that the top will crisp and brown quickly and evenly, while the food beneath the top layer will not dry out. The Gratin's smooth interior enamel does not require greasing before cooking pastry crusts.

• One particularly useful benefit of Le Creuset's enameled cast iron Gratin is its capability and performance on the grill or stovetop, making it the right tool for the job when deglazing. After the meat is cooked, the caramelized sugars and bits of remaining food can be removed and dissolved with stock or wine to make a pan sauce or gravy.

Quiche Lorraine

A good quiche makes an ideal dish for a picnic, buffet, or any casual entertaining with family or friends. In this recipe, the cheese flavor is enhanced by adding it to the pie crust as well as the filling. Try the method described here of making the dough with a few tablespoons of milk because it makes a pastry with a very light, crisp texture.

SERVES: 4
PREPARATION TIME: 10 minutes for the pie-crust dough, plus 1½–2 hours resting time, and 5 minutes to make the filling
COOKING TIME: 35–40 minutes
COOK IN: a 1 quart au gratin dish

INGREDIENTS

for the pie crust:

1 cup all-purpose flour, plus extra for dusting
pinch of salt
½ stick cold butter, diced
⅓ cup finely grated mature Cheddar cheese
2–3 tablespoons milk

for the filling:

1 teaspoon olive oil
3½ oz lean bacon, diced
1 cup finely grated mature Cheddar cheese
3 extra large eggs
1 cup crème fraîche or sour cream
½ teaspoon black pepper
1 tablespoon snipped chives

1. Put the flour, salt, and butter into a bowl. Using your fingertips or a pastry blender, work the butter into the flour until it resembles coarse breadcrumbs. Stir in the cheese and milk, and work the mixture into a dough.

2. Turn out the dough onto a floured surface and knead gently until smooth. Wrap in plastic wrap and leave to stand at room temperature for 30 minutes to 1 hour.

3. Roll out the dough on a floured surface until it is large enough to line the bottom and sides of the dish. Line the dish with the pie crust. Cover and chill for at least 1 hour.

4. Preheat the oven to 375°F.

5. To make the filling, heat the olive oil in a small frying pan, cook the diced bacon until crisp, and then drain. Spread half the cheese over the pastry-lined au gratin dish. Add the cooked bacon and the remaining cheese.

6. Beat together the eggs, crème fraîche or sour cream, and black pepper. Pour this over the filling and sprinkle with the chopped chives.

7. Bake in the center of the oven for 20 minutes. Reduce the temperature to 325°F and then continue cooking for a further 15–20 minutes or until the filling is set and the top pale golden brown.

8. Leave to cool for 10–15 minutes before serving—a quiche is at its best when warm and not piping hot.

COOKING TIP

For a party-size quiche to serve 12 people, use the 3 quart au gratin dish, triple the ingredient quantities, and increase the cooking time from 15–20 minutes to 35–40 minutes when you reduce the temperature in Step 7.

Honey-Glazed Pork Chops

The honey in this recipe really enhances the flavor of the pork to create a quick and easy supper dish. Serve with creamy mash potatoes or plain rice and some fresh vegetables or a salad.

SERVES: 2
PREPARATION TIME: 5 minutes, plus 1 hour marinating time
COOKING TIME: about 20 minutes
COOK IN: a 3 quart au gratin dish

INGREDIENTS
2 boneless pork loin chops, 1in thick
1 tablespoon oil
salt and freshly ground black pepper
1 cup chicken stock
½ teaspoon cornstarch mixed with a little water to make a paste
rosemary sprigs, to garnish

for the marinade:
1 tablespoon honey
1 tablespoon red wine vinegar
1 teaspoon Dijon mustard
1 garlic clove, crushed
1 teaspoon chopped fresh rosemary

1. To make the marinade, mix together the honey, wine vinegar, mustard, garlic, and rosemary. Place the chops in a dish and pour over the marinade. Cover and leave in a cool place to marinate for 1 hour, turning from time to time.

2. Preheat the oven to 425°F. Pour the oil into the au gratin dish and heat on top of the stove. Remove the chops from the marinade, season with salt and pepper, and place them in the dish. Brown the chops on both sides, and then transfer the dish to the oven and bake for about 12 minutes until cooked through.

3. Transfer the chops to heated plates and keep warm. Place the dish on the stove on a medium heat and pour in the chicken stock. Allow it to bubble, stirring with a wooden spoon and scraping the dish to dissolve any sediment.

4. Stir in the cornstarch, cook for a minute until thickened, and then pour over the chops. Serve garnished with rosemary.

COOKING TIP

The ingredients in this recipe can easily be doubled up to serve 4 people.

Scallops à La Provençal

This scallop dish is simple to prepare and cook. Recipes may vary, but they traditionally include the base ingredients of olive oil, garlic, tomatoes, and white wine. Serve with toasted French bread and a crisp green salad.

SERVES: 6
PREPARATION TIME: 10 minutes
COOKING TIME: 10 minutes
COOK IN: a 3 quart au gratin dish

INGREDIENTS

1½ lb bay or sea scallops
salt and freshly ground black pepper
4 tablespoons all-purpose flour
2 tablespoons olive oil
4 large or 6 small shallots, finely chopped
4 garlic cloves, minced
3 tablespoons butter
½ cup dry white wine, at room temperature
2 plum tomatoes, diced
3 tablespoons chopped fresh parsley
lemon wedges, to serve

1. Season the scallops with a little salt and pepper, and toss in the flour to coat lightly, dusting off any excess.

2. Warm the olive oil in the dish over a low to medium heat on the stove. Add the chopped shallots and garlic, and gently fry without coloring for 2–3 minutes. Remove with a draining spoon onto a plate, retaining any oil in the dish, and set to one side.

3. Melt the butter along with the retained olive oil in the dish. Once bubbling, add the scallops individually and lightly brown on both sides, taking care not to overheat the dish or the butter may burn.

4. Return the onions and garlic to the pan and stir in the white wine and tomatoes, and then continue to cook for 3–4 minutes to allow the sauce to thicken and reduce a little.

5. Adjust the seasoning to taste and sprinkle over the chopped parsley. Serve with the lemon wedges.

COOKING TIPS

The dish can also be made in a 1¾ quart skillet.

If the scallops are very large, cut them in half horizontally.

Always add the scallops individually to the pan and do not overcrowd them or the end result will be steamed rather than seared. Scallops should be opaque in the center when they are ready; overcooking will make them tough.

Potato Dauphinoise

In France, this dish is called "gratin dauphinoise." It is an excellent potato dish for a large family gathering or a celebration meal because it is flexible and can be prepared in advance and baked later. Waxy potatoes give the best result because they hold their shape well.

SERVES: 8–10
PREPARATION TIME: 25 minutes
COOKING TIME: 40–45 minutes, plus parboiling the potatoes
COOK IN: a 3 quart au gratin dish

INGREDIENTS
3lb 5oz waxy potatoes, peeled
1 large garlic clove, halved
1 tablespoon butter, softened
¼ teaspoon freshly grated nutmeg
salt and freshly ground black pepper
1 cup finely grated Gruyère cheese
1 cup heavy cream
½ cup milk

1. Cut the potatoes into ¼in slices. Put them into a large saucepan on the stove, cover with cold water, add a little salt, and bring to a boil on a high heat. Reduce the heat and simmer for 2 minutes. Do not overcook at this stage because even waxy potatoes can begin to break up. Drain well.

2. Rub the inside of the au gratin dish with the cut garlic and grease with a little of the butter.

3. Preheat the oven to 325°F. Put half the potatoes in the dish, spreading them out evenly. Sprinkle with a little of the nutmeg and some salt and pepper. Add half the cheese and then another layer of potatoes, nutmeg, and a little more salt and pepper.

4. Beat together the cream and milk, and pour the mixture evenly over the potatoes. Finish by scattering the remaining cheese on top with a few small pieces of butter dotted over the surface.

5. Bake in the center of the oven for 40–45 minutes until a deep, crisp, brown crust forms. Serve immediately from the dish.

COOKING TIPS

The recipe can also be made in a 2⅜ quart skillet or the base of a 3½ quart braiser.

You can make the recipe in advance up to the end of Step 4 and then bake when the dish is required.

For a healthier alternative, low-fat cream and milk can be used instead.

Crème Brulée with Berries

Au gratin dishes have endless uses for a range of delicious savory and sweet dishes. An au gratin dish is especially useful for making crème brulée because it can bake gently in the oven and then withstand the high heat of the broiler for finishing off the dish.

SERVES: 6
PREPARATION TIME: 30 minutes
COOKING TIME: 1 hour 10 minutes, plus overnight chilling for the base, and 2–3 hours cooling for the caramel topping
COOK IN: a 1 quart au gratin dish

INGREDIENTS
2½ cups heavy cream
1 vanilla bean
4 egg yolks
½ cup superfine sugar

for the berries:
5½ oz raspberries
2–3 tablespoons powdered sugar
1½ cups mixed summer berries (such as strawberries, raspberries, blackberries, and blueberries)

1. Preheat the oven to 300°F. Place the cream in a saucepan. Slit the vanilla bean and scrape the seeds into the cream. Add the scraped bean. Heat gently to just below simmering point.

2. Meanwhile, whisk together the egg yolks and half the sugar in a bowl. Whisk in the hot cream. Remove the vanilla bean and pour the custard into the au gratin dish. Place the dish in a roaster and pour in boiling water to come halfway up the sides of the au gratin dish. Bake in the oven for about 1 hour or until set. Leave to cool, and then cover and place in the refrigerator overnight.

3. Preheat a broiler. Sprinkle the remaining sugar over the surface of the custard. Broil for 2–3 minutes until the sugar melts and caramelizes. Allow 2–3 hours to cool until the caramel topping is firm and crisp.

4. Meanwhile, place the raspberries in a pan with 1 tablespoon of water and heat gently until they start to release their juice. Place in a blender or food-processor and blend to a purée. Press through a sieve into a bowl. Sweeten to taste with the powdered sugar.

5. Cut the strawberries in half or quarters, depending on their size, and add to the raspberry purée along with the other summer berries.

6. Serve the crème brulée with the summer berries.

COOKING TIP

If you wish, you may use a blowtorch to melt and caramelize the sugar in Step 3.

Roasters

Background

With its deep sides, the Le Creuset enameled cast iron Roaster allows for precisely the correct amount of crisping and browning while also containing fat and juices that can splatter during cooking.

Cooking with Roasters

The even heat distribution of our versatile enameled cast iron Roasters makes them ideal for oven-roasted chicken breasts, homemade lasagne, casseroles, and even a side of roasted new potatoes. When roasting meat, the dish can be placed on the stovetop for deglazing a gravy or sauce. After draining away the excess fat, the caramelized sugars and bits of remaining food can be removed and dissolved with stock or wine to make a pan sauce or gravy. They are also perfect for use directly on an outdoor grill.

The True Benefit of Le Creuset

With the durable properties of cast iron and the ability to go from the oven to the refrigerator or freezer without warping, Le Creuset enameled cast iron Roasters are perfect for storing and reheating leftovers from family dinners, parties or holiday meals. They also make ideal serving dishes with their full and even heating, keeping food warmer longer at the table.

Cooking Tips

• Allow at least a two-inch gap all around the roasting dish once it is placed in the oven, ensuring the correct flow of heat can circulate for more even cooking results.

• Due to their cast iron construction, Le Creuset enameled cast iron Roasters retain heat very effectively, meaning oven temperatures should rarely exceed 350ºF while cooking.

Slow-Roasted Pork Shoulder

Slow roasting a shoulder of pork for lunch or a dinner party ensures tender meat and crisp crackling. Roasting the joint on a rack in the roasting dish allows heat to circulate efficiently and fat to drain away.

SERVES: 8
PREPARATION TIME: 15 minutes
COOKING TIME: 6 hours
COOK IN: a 5¼ quart roaster with a roasting rack

INGREDIENTS
4½ lb boned and rolled shoulder of pork (with the rind on)
2 garlic cloves, cut into slivers
2 tablespoons brown sugar
1 tablespoon sea salt
1 teaspoon coarsely crushed black peppercorns
1 teaspoon fennel seeds, crushed
1 onion, finely chopped
2 carrots, peeled and finely chopped

for the tomato sauce:
14oz can chopped tomatoes
⅔ cup red wine
chicken stock, as needed

1. Preheat the oven to 425°F. Score the pork rind thoroughly with slashes quite close together. Insert the garlic slivers into the slashes. Mix together the sugar, salt, pepper, and fennel seeds, and rub over the meat, rubbing the mixture well into the scores in the skin. Place on the rack in the roaster. Roast in the oven for 30 minutes.

2. Remove from the oven. Drain off any fat and cover the roaster with aluminum foil. Reduce the oven temperature to 325°F and return the pork to the oven for a further 4½ hours.

3. Carefully remove the pork and rack from the roaster. Pour off most of the fat. Place the roaster on the stove, add the onion and carrots, and cook gently in the fat for a few minutes.

4. To make the sauce, stir in the tomatoes and wine. Replace the pork and rack in the roaster. Cover with foil and roast for a further 30 minutes. Remove the foil and continue roasting for 30 minutes. If the tomato mixture in the base of the tin appears to be too dry, add some chicken stock.

5. If, at the end of the cooking time, the crackling on the pork is not completely crisp, increase the oven temperature and return the meat to the oven for a few more minutes.

6. Serve the pork with the tomato sauce.

COOKING TIPS

Ask your butcher to score the pork rind for you.

If a smooth sauce is preferred, press the tomato mixture through a sieve and add a little more stock, if necessary.

Serve the pork with potatoes roasted in the pork fat removed from the roaster.

Lasagne Verdi alla Bolognese

Traditional Italian lasagne is made up of layers of beef Bolognese and béchamel sauce interleaved with pasta sheets, finished with Parmesan cheese, and baked until crispy and brown. This recipe uses pasta verdi which is a green pasta that derives its color from the addition of spinach. It takes time, care, and a little love to produce this wonderful dish, which should stand proudly on the plate.

SERVES: 6
PREPARATION TIME: 30 minutes
COOKING TIME: 2 hours, plus cooking time for the pasta
COOK IN: a 2½ quart roaster

INGREDIENTS

12 sheets of lasagne verdi (cooked as recommended on the packet)
1 cup grated Parmesan cheese, to finish

for the Bolognese sauce:

2 tablespoons olive oil
½ cup diced pancetta
1 onion, diced
1 celery stick, diced
1 carrot, diced
2 garlic cloves, minced
1lb ground beef chuck steak
1 cup red wine, at room temperature
2 cups beef stock
14oz can chopped tomatoes
2 tablespoons tomato paste
½–1 teaspoon black pepper
1 bouquet garni (made up of a sprig each of fresh rosemary and thyme, 2 sage and bay leaves, and a few parsley stalks)

for the béchamel sauce:

½ stick butter
scant ½ cup all-purpose flour
3 cups milk
¼ teaspoon ground nutmeg
1 cup grated Parmesan cheese

1. To make the Bolognese sauce, heat the oil in a large wide-based pan over a moderate heat, add the pancetta, and cook for 2–3 minutes. Stir in the diced vegetables and garlic, and sweat for 5–6 minutes, stirring so that they do not brown.

2. Add the ground beef and allow to sear for 2 minutes before stirring and breaking up the meat. A large silicone spatula is ideal for this. Once all the beef is browned, add the remaining ingredients, stir well to remove any caramelized pieces from the base of the pan, bring to a gentle simmer, and cook uncovered for 40–45 minutes. The Bolognese sauce will be thick and the meat tender when ready. Stir occasionally and add a little water if the sauce becomes too dry towards the end of the cooking time.

3. Preheat the oven to 375°F.

4. To make the béchamel sauce, melt the butter in a saucepan, add the flour, and cook for a couple of minutes. Remove from the heat and whisk in the milk a little at a time. Add the nutmeg and Parmesan cheese, place back over the heat, and whisk until thick and glossy.

5. To make up the lasagne, spread a quarter of the Bolognese sauce over the base of the dish and cover with 3 sheets of the cooked pasta. Spread a second layer of Bolognese sauce, adding a thin layer of béchamel sauce, and cover with 3 sheets of pasta. Repeat with two more layers of Bolognese sauce, béchamel sauce, and sheets of pasta, and finish with a final thick layer of béchamel sauce.

6. Sprinkle over the Parmesan cheese and bake in the oven for 35–40 minutes.

7. Allow to stand for 10 minutes before serving. This will allow the lasagne to firm up, thus making serving easier.

Roasted Stuffed Peppers

SERVES: 6 as a snack and 3 as a main course
PREPARATION TIME: 15 minutes
COOKING TIME: 45–50 minutes
COOK IN: a 2½ quart roaster

INGREDIENTS
3 large red or orange bell peppers
2 teaspoons olive oil, plus extra for greasing
1 onion, finely chopped
1lb lean ground beef steak
14oz can chopped tomatoes
2 garlic cloves, finely chopped
⅓ cup uncooked long-grain white rice
1 tablespoon Worcestershire sauce
1 tablespoon chopped fresh oregano
1 tablespoon chopped fresh parsley
a few drops of Tabasco or chili sauce (optional)
salt and freshly ground black pepper

for the topping:
1 cup white breadcrumbs
1 cup grated Cheddar cheese
2 tablespoons melted butter

Roasting vegetables, such as peppers, has probably been one of the fastest growing trends in cooking over recent years. We are all encouraged to eat more fresh vegetables and this is without a doubt a delicious way in which to do so.

1. Cut the peppers in half horizontally through the stem end, leaving the pieces of stem attached but removing the seeds and any white membrane. Cook the rice in advance.

2. In a frying pan, gently fry the onion in the olive oil over a medium heat until translucent, add the ground beef, and stir-fry for a few minutes to brown. Add the chopped tomatoes and simmer for 8–10 minutes. Remove from the heat.

3. Preheat the oven to 375°F.

4. Mix the garlic, cooked rice, Worcestershire sauce, fresh herbs, and Tabasco or chili sauce (if using) into the ground beef mixture. Season to taste with salt and black pepper. Spoon this mixture into the pepper shells, packing it down a little because it will shrink when roasted.

5. Mix the breadcrumbs together with the grated cheese and melted butter. Top the stuffed peppers with the breadcrumb mixture, pressing it down firmly to make sure that it stays inside the peppers. Lightly brush the roasting dish with some olive oil and put in the filled peppers.

6. Roast in the oven for 45–50 minutes until the peppers are tender and the topping is golden brown.

COOKING TIPS

The recipe can also be made in the base of a 2¼ quart braiser or a 3 quart au gratin dish.

The same filling can be used to stuff zucchini shells or scooped-out eggplant halves. Finely chop the scooped-out flesh and add it to the stuffing.

Vegetable Tian

This recipe is made with a medley of Mediterranean vegetables marinated in basil-infused olive oil and baked with a topping of Parmesan cheese. It makes a good accompaniment to poultry or fish; alternatively, it can be served simply with warm crusty bread. Allow to cool a little before eating as the flavors are at their best when it is eaten warm rather that hot.

SERVES: 8 as an accompaniment
PREPARATION TIME: 15 minutes, plus 1 hour marinating time
COOKING TIME: 50 minutes
COOK IN: a 2½ quart roaster

INGREDIENTS
scant ½ cup basil-infused olive oil
2 garlic cloves, finely chopped
½ teaspoon black pepper
½ teaspoon coarse sea salt
1 tablespoon chopped fresh thyme
1 tablespoon chopped fresh parsley
2 medium zucchini, cut into ¼ in slices
2 small eggplants, cut into ¼ in slices
3 large tomatoes, cut into ¼ in slices
1 tablespoon olive oil
2 onions, finely sliced
2 cups freshly grated Parmesan cheese

1. Preheat the oven to 350°F. Mix together the basil oil, garlic, seasoning, and chopped herbs in a very large bowl. Add the sliced zucchini, eggplants, and tomatoes, and coat well in the oil mixture. Cover tightly with plastic wrap and allow to marinate for 1 hour. During the marinating time, give the bowl a couple of good shakes to help distribute the marinade among the vegetables.

2. Add the olive oil to the roaster and heat on top of the stove over a medium heat.

3. Add the sliced onion and fry gently until softened but not brown (this will take about 4–5 minutes). Remove the roaster from the heat.

4. Spread the cooked onion evenly over the base of the roaster.

5. Layer the oil-infused vegetables upright in lines, starting with the eggplants, followed by a second line of tomatoes, and then a third line of zucchini, overlapping the vegetables as you go. Repeat the layering process until all the vegetables have been used up. (Don't worry if it's not perfectly neat because this will add to the rustic appearance of the dish.)

6. Pour over any marinade left in the bowl and top with the grated Parmesan cheese.

7. Bake in the oven for 45 minutes until the vegetables are tender and the top is golden brown in color.

COOKING TIPS

The recipe can also be made in a 3 quart oval au gratin dish.

Basil-infused olive oil is available in most supermarkets. If you prefer, you can use a good-quality plain olive oil instead.

Grated Gruyère cheese can be used in place of the Parmesan.

Roasted Root Vegetables

Roasting brings out the natural sweetness of root vegetables such as parsnips, turnips, and carrots, while the cast-iron roaster ensures that they will cook evenly with lovely caramelized edges.

SERVES: 6
PREPARATION TIME: 15 minutes
COOKING TIME: 45 minutes
COOK IN: a 5¼ quart roaster

INGREDIENTS
10oz fingerling potatoes
6 small carrots
2 parsnips
3 small turnips
12 shallots
4 garlic cloves
a fresh rosemary sprig
a fresh thyme sprig
salt and freshly ground black pepper
2 tablespoons olive oil
1 tablespoon honey

1. Preheat the oven to 400°F. Wash the potatoes, but do not peel them. Cut them in half, lengthwise, and place them in the roaster.

2. Peel the carrots, parsnips, and turnips, and cut them into pieces that are of a similar size to the potatoes. Add to the potatoes.

3. Peel the shallots and garlic, and add to the vegetables along with the rosemary and thyme. Season with salt and pepper. Stir in the olive oil and toss together. Roast in the oven for about 45 minutes, turning once, until the vegetables are tender and golden.

4. Stir in the honey about 5 minutes before the end of the cooking time.

COOKING TIPS

Fingerling potatoes are small, long, narrow potatoes with a firm yellow flesh. If they are not available, choose another waxy variety such as Charlotte or Pink Fir Apple.

The mixture of root vegetables in this dish can be varied according to taste. The total quantity of prepared vegetables should be about 2¼ lb. Sweet potato, beets, celeriac, Jerusalem artichokes, and squash all roast beautifully.

Tiramisù

The title of this popular Italian dessert literally means "pick me up." The recipe given here is a slightly simplified version of the traditional one, which contains raw egg yolk, because more and more people have an intolerance to raw or lightly cooked eggs. However, the resulting tiramisù will still have a firm consistency that can be cut into squares. It is generously laced with brandy, but rum or Italian Marsala wine can also be used.

SERVES: 10
PREPARATION TIME: 20 minutes, plus 5–6 hours chilling time
COOKING TIME: 8–10 minutes for the ladyfinger biscuits
COOK IN: a 2½ quart roaster

INGREDIENTS
40 ladyfinger biscuits
1 lb mascarpone cheese
⅓ cup sugar
1 cup heavy cream, beaten lightly
⅓ cup brandy
4 cups strong black coffee
2 tablespoons unsweetened cocoa powder, sifted

1. Lightly bake the ladyfinger biscuits at 350°F for 8–10 minutes, and allow to cool before using.

2. Beat the cheese and sugar together until light and fluffy. Add the cream and brandy, beating these lightly, but not so much that the mixture becomes too stiff: it should have a soft dropping consistency.

3. Pour the coffee into a flat bowl, such as a pie plate. Dip the biscuits very quickly into the coffee. Make a single layer in the bottom of the roaster, using half the biscuits.

4. Spread over half the cheese mixture, add the second layer of dipped biscuits, and finally add the second layer of cheese. Using a round-bladed knife, make a scrolled-line pattern over the cheese mixture. Cover with plastic wrap and chill for 5–6 hours.

5. Before serving, sprinkle the cocoa powder liberally over the surface.

COOKING TIP

When entertaining, this recipe can be made 1 or 2 days in advance to the end of Step 4, then covered tightly, and chilled until required. Do not add the cocoa powder until the day the dessert is to be served.

Woks

Background

Originally conceived to rest over a pit-style stove, the wok has been a staple of East Asian cuisine for centuries. Woks are typically used for stir-frying, and their rounded, narrow bases allow for quickly cooking large quantities of meat and vegetables with very little oil.

Cooking with Woks

Our classic Asian-inspired design is perfectly weight-balanced with a flat base and sloping sides, and features a smooth, gently curved interior cooking surface for stir-frying fresh ingredients.

The True Benefit of Le Creuset

The Le Creuset Wok with Glass Lid combines the traditional curved cooking surface of thinner, round-bottomed woks with a flat base that ensures solid contact with any stovetop heat source, including electric and induction. Its glass lid gives it multi-functional capability for techniques like braising, boiling, steaming, and frying in addition to traditional open stir-frying.

Cooking Tips

• When stir-frying for several people, save time by pre-blanching crisp vegetables for about one minute before finishing in the wok.

• The wok's concave shape allows for maximum control during preparation—so larger ingredients can be seared quickly and moved up the side to finish cooking while other ingredients are added and cooked at high heat in the oil at the bottom.

Beef and Sugar Snap Pea Stir-Fry

Stir-fries are quick and easy to prepare and cook, making them ideal for a healthy evening meal when you are short of time. Crisp, slightly crunchy vegetables, such as sugar snap peas and scallions, taste delicious with the succulent pieces of beef.

SERVES: 4 when served with additional dishes
PREPARATION TIME: 15 minutes, plus 15 minutes marinating time
COOKING TIME: 8 minutes
COOK IN: a 4¾ quart wok

INGREDIENTS

10oz top rump or flank steak
1 egg white
4 tablespoons soy sauce
1 tablespoon cornstarch
3 tablespoons oil
1 red chili, deseeded and cut into fine rings
1in piece fresh root ginger, peeled and grated
2 garlic cloves, crushed
6 scallions, sliced diagonally
6oz sugar snap peas
2 tablespoons oyster sauce
½ teaspoon sugar
boiled rice or egg noodles, to serve

1. Cut the steak, across the grain, into very thin strips, about 1½–2in long. In a bowl, whisk together the egg white, 1 tablespoon of the soy sauce, and the cornstarch. Add the beef and toss to coat thoroughly. Leave to marinate for 15 minutes.

2. Heat 2 tablespoons of the oil in the wok. Add the beef and cook quickly until lightly browned. Set aside on a plate.

3. Heat the remaining oil in the wok and add the chili, ginger, garlic, and scallions. Stir-fry for 1 minute.

4. Add the sugar snap peas and stir-fry for 1 minute.

5. Add the remaining soy sauce, the oyster sauce, and the sugar.

6. Return the beef to the wok, stir everything together, and then serve with plain boiled rice or egg noodles.

COOKING TIP

The ingredients in this recipe can be doubled to serve 4 people as a main course.

Braised Orange Duck

Chinese braising, like stir-frying, is an excellent way to cook a meal in a wok. The long, slow cooking of the duck on a bed of vegetables and orange zest results in a very tender dish, full of intense flavors. The parboiling of the duck removes a considerable amount of its fat and helps to make the meat very tender.

SERVES: 6
PREPARATION TIME: 10 minutes, plus 15 minutes boiling
COOKING TIME: 3–3½ hours
COOK IN: a 4¾ quart wok

INGREDIENTS
6 duck legs
2 tablespoons peanut oil
6 scallions, trimmed and roughly chopped
6 shallots, quartered
3 medium carrots, cut into finger-size pieces
zest of 2 large oranges
2 tablespoons dark soy sauce
4 tablespoons orange juice
1 level teaspoon Chinese five–spice powder
4 star anise
freshly ground black pepper
boiled rice, to serve

1. Trim the duck of excess skin or fat, or remove the skin completely if you prefer. Put all the duck pieces into the wok, cover with boiling water, and bring to a boil. Reduce the heat, cover with the wok lid, and simmer gently for 15 minutes. Remove the duck and discard the cooking liquid. Dry the duck on kitchen paper.

2. Rinse and dry the wok. Heat the oil in the wok over a medium heat. Add the duck, a few pieces at a time, and brown evenly on both sides. Remove the duck with a slotted spoon, draining well.

3. When all the duck is browned, add the vegetables to the hot oil and stir-fry for 2–3 minutes until they begin to soften and color.

4. Return the duck pieces to the wok on top of the vegetables. Add the orange zest, all the remaining ingredients, and 4 tablespoons of water, pushing the star anise and orange zest down between the duck pieces.

5. Cover the wok and cook over a very low heat on the stove for 3–3½ hours until the duck is very tender and the vegetables have almost reached a purée. Remove the orange zest and star anise pieces before serving. Serve with some boiled rice.

COOKING TIPS

The recipe can also be made in the 3½ quart braiser.

Chicken leg quarters can also be used for this recipe. They do not require boiling, and only need 2–2½ hours cooking time.

Steamed Sea Bass with Noodles

This is a typically Eastern way to cook fish. It results in the fish being plump and moist, and gently perfumed with the flavors of lemon grass and ginger. The generous size of the wok allows sufficient room for a steaming rack to hold the fish above the gently simmering liquid.

SERVES: 2
PREPARATION TIME: 10 minutes
COOKING TIME: 15 minutes
COOK IN: a 4¾ quart wok

INGREDIENTS

1lb sea bass (about 2 small fish), cleaned
1in piece fresh root ginger, peeled and very thinly sliced
2 tablespoons chopped fresh flat-leaf parsley
3 pieces lemon grass
2 teaspoons light soy sauce
4½ oz dried fine egg noodles

1. Remove the fins, tail, and head of the fish, if preferred. Cut two deep slashes into both sides of the fish and push a few pieces of the ginger and a little of the parsley into the slashes. Cut the lemon grass lengthwise and put a small piece inside the cavity of each fish.

2. Pour 2 cups of water and a piece of lemon grass into the wok over a medium heat on the stove. Bring to a boil and then reduce to a gentle simmer. Position the steaming rack in the wok.

3. Place the fish on the rack, scatter over the remaining pieces of lemon grass, and sprinkle with 1 teaspoon of the soy sauce. Cover and steam for 8–10 minutes.

4. Uncover the wok and carefully lift up the rack holding the fish. Add the dried noodles to the liquid with the remaining chopped parsley. Return the rack and fish to the wok, re-cover, and cook for a further 3–4 minutes.

5. Remove the fish from the wok and discard the lemon grass. Drain the noodles, discarding the lemon grass.

6. Serve the fish on top of the noodles with the remaining soy sauce sprinkled over the top.

COOKING TIPS

Light soy sauce is more salty than dark, so do not add salt to the recipe until after you have tasted it.

Other small whole fish, such as trout or small sea salmon, can also be used in this recipe.

A Pinot Gris or Muscat from the Alsace region of France are the top choices for this dish. Both will work well with the ginger and lemon grass.

Vegetable Tempura with Sweet-and-Sour Sauce

SERVES: 6 as an appetizer
PREPARATION TIME: 25 minutes, plus 10 minutes for the sauce
COOKING TIME: 15 minutes
COOK IN: a 4¾ quart wok

It is important that the wok is not overfilled with the frying oil when you cook this dish because, as the ingredients are added, the level rises and any excess water in them can cause spitting. This tempura batter uses carbonated water, which gives a much lighter result than either milk or water.

INGREDIENTS

for the sweet-and-sour sauce:

2 tablespoons peanut oil
2 shallots, finely chopped
1 garlic clove, finely minced
3 tablespoons dark soy sauce
2 tablespoons tomato paste
3 tablespoons honey
½ cup fresh orange juice
1½ teaspoons freshly ground black pepper
1½ teaspoons cornstarch

for the batter:

1 cup all-purpose flour
½ teaspoon salt
1 teaspoon ground hot chili powder
1 egg, beaten
1 cup carbonated water

for the vegetables:

3 cups peanut or vegetable oil, for frying (divided)
9oz broccoli, broken into florets
9oz zucchini, cut into 2in finger-size pieces
9oz sweet potato, peeled, cut in half lengthwise, and then cut into ⅛in thick slices
lime wedges, to garnish

1. To make the sauce, heat the oil in a small saucepan over a medium heat. Add the shallots and garlic, and fry gently until the shallots are soft. Stir in all of the remaining ingredients, except for the cornstarch, and add 4 tablespoons of water.

2. Simmer for 10 minutes. Blend the cornstarch with a little water and stir into the sauce. Continue simmering and stirring until the sauce is thick. Cook for 1 minute, remove from the heat, and add seasoning to taste.

3. To make the batter, put the flour, salt, and chili powder into a bowl. Add the egg and half the carbonated water, and beat until smooth. Stir in the remaining carbonated water.

4. Heat 2 cups of the oil in the wok to 350°F, or until a piece of bread dropped into the oil rises to the surface and is golden brown in 30 seconds. (For extra safety when deep-frying, use an oil thermometer to check the temperature.)

5. In batches, dip the vegetables into the batter, shake off any excess, and drop in the hot oil.

6. Fry the vegetables for 2–3 minutes until the batter is puffed up and pale golden brown; the vegetables should still have a little "bite" to them. Drain as they are ready on a tempura rack resting on the wok rim to keep hot.

7. About halfway through the frying process, skim away and discard any batter residues and top up with the remaining 1 cup of oil. Check the oil temperature as per Step 4 before continuing frying. (Discard the frying oil after use because it will contain pieces of batter.)

8. Reheat the sauce and divide among 3 small dishes so that two guests can share a dish. Serve the tempura with the dipping sauce.

Tagines

Background

This authentic cooking vessel from the Mediterranean and Atlantic coasts of North Africa promotes natural steam circulation inside its cone-shaped lid to keep beef, lamb, and other meats perfectly tender and exceptionally flavorful.

Cooking with Tagines

Traditional Moroccan tagines (the dish is named for the cookware) typically include a combination of braised meat (often lamb, beef, or chicken), fruits, root vegetables, and fragrant spices like cinnamon, saffron, and ginger.

The True Benefit of Le Creuset

Inspired by the slowly simmered, heavily seasoned cuisines indigenous to North Africa, the Moroccan tagine is a classic example of form following function. Its distinctive lid allows for the constant return of condensation to the base, moistening ingredients and tenderizing tough fibers within the meat. And because it's crafted from durable cast iron, the tagine retains heat longer and cooks food more evenly and thoroughly.

Cooking Tips

- Tagines are intended for stovetop use only, as the lid would become too hot inside the oven and the moisture in the food would evaporate instead of condensing.

- The Le Creuset Tagine's versatile cast iron base features a satin black enamel cooking surface that is not only suitable for browning on the stovetop, but also warming tortillas in the oven when used separately from the stoneware lid.

White Fish Tagine with Couscous

SERVES: 4
PREPARATION TIME: 10 minutes, plus 30 minutes marinating time
COOKING TIME: 1¼–1½ hours
COOK IN: a 2 quart tagine

INGREDIENTS
2¼ lb firm white fish (such as cod, monkfish, or halibut)

for the marinade:
1 small red chili, deseeded and finely chopped
2 garlic cloves, crushed
1 teaspoon ground coriander
1 teaspoon ground cumin
1 teaspoon turmeric
2 tablespoons olive oil
finely grated zest of 1 lemon
4 tablespoons lemon juice

for the sauce:
2 tablespoons olive oil
1 small onion, coarsely chopped
12oz eggplant, cut into ½in cubes
1 potato, peeled and cut into ½in cubes
1lb canned plum tomatoes, chopped with their juice
1 teaspoon tomato paste
2 tablespoons chopped fresh cilantro
salt and freshly ground black pepper
⅓ cup pitted green olives

for the couscous, to serve:
2 cups couscous
2 cups boiling water or chicken stock
2 teaspoons olive oil

Not all tagine recipes have to cook for hours, and this spicy vegetable sauce is only cooked for about an hour before the fish is added. If it is more convenient, the sauce can be made in advance and then reheated with whatever fresh fish you are serving.

1. Mix together all the marinade ingredients in an au gratin dish or a non-metallic bowl. Cut the fish into large chunks and add it to the marinade, gently turning it so that it is evenly coated. Cover and leave to marinate in the refrigerator for 30 minutes.

2. Heat the oil for the sauce in the tagine base over a medium heat on the stove. Add the onion, eggplant, and potato, and fry until they are just beginning to color and become soft.

3. Add the tomatoes and their juice with the tomato paste. Add 1 tablespoon of the cilantro and some seasoning. Cover with the lid and cook over a very low heat for 1–1¼ hours until the vegetables are tender.

4. To prepare the couscous, put it into a large bowl, pour over the boiling water or stock, cover with a plate, and leave to stand for 10 minutes. Add the olive oil and stir to separate the grains.

5. Transfer the couscous to a fine-mesh strainer or colander lined with a piece of cheesecloth. Place over a saucepan or casserole filled with hot water, cover, and steam for 10–15 minutes to heat through. Season with a little salt and pepper before serving.

6. While the couscous is cooking, add the fish to the sauce, together with any remaining marinade and the olives. Re-cover the tagine and cook for a further 10–15 minutes until the fish is cooked.

7. Sprinkle with the remaining cilantro and serve with the steamed couscous.

COOKING TIP

The recipe can also be made in a 2½ quart braiser.

Lamb Shanks with Okra

This recipe is typical of the North African style of tagine cooking, using very little liquid to moisten the ingredients at the beginning and allowing the natural meat and vegetable juices to be released as the dish slowly cooks. Lamb shanks are sold in supermarkets, but any lean lamb that is cut into large chunks may be used instead.

SERVES: 4
PREPARATION TIME: 20 minutes
COOKING TIME: 3½–4 hours
COOK IN: a 2 quart tagine

INGREDIENTS
2 tablespoons olive oil
1 large red onion, thinly sliced
3 small mild red chilies, deseeded and chopped
2 garlic cloves, chopped
4 lamb shanks, trimmed of fat
2 teaspoons ground cumin
2 teaspoons ground coriander
1 teaspoon ground turmeric
1lb canned plum tomatoes, chopped with their juice
¼ teaspoon salt
a pinch of freshly ground black pepper
4½ oz fresh okra
1 tablespoon chopped fresh flat-leaf parsley, to garnish

for the couscous, to serve:
2 cups couscous
2 cups boiling water or chicken stock
2 teaspoons olive oil

1. Heat the oil in the tagine base over a medium heat on top of the stove. Add the onion and fry until it begins to soften and color. Add the chilies and garlic, and fry for a further minute. Remove with a slotted spoon, draining well.

2. Add the lamb shanks, two at a time, and brown evenly. Remove each one as it becomes brown.

3. Return the onion mixture to the tagine, stir in the spices, and cook slowly for 1 minute, stirring continuously. Mix in the tomatoes and their juice.

4. Lay the lamb shanks on top (in two layers if necessary). Spoon some of the sauce over them and season with the salt and pepper.

5. Cover with the tagine lid and simmer over a very low heat for 3–3½ hours until the lamb shanks are tender, rearranging them after half the time so that the ones on the top go to the bottom.

6. When the lamb is tender, push the okra in around the meat and cook for a further 30–40 minutes.

7. Before serving, sprinkle with the chopped parsley. Serve with plain steamed couscous (see page 128, Steps 4 and 5).

COOKING TIPS

The recipe can also be made in a 3½ quart braiser or a large, round or oval French oven.

Do not touch your face, particularly your eyes, after handling and cutting chilies because they contain a powerful irritant. Wash your hands, the board, and the knife thoroughly.

Moroccan Chicken Tagine

SERVES: 4
PREPARATION TIME: 30 minutes, plus 6 hours marinating time
COOKING TIME: 2¼ hours
COOK IN: a 2 quart tagine

Combining fruit with meat, poultry, or fish is typical of North African cuisine, and with a spicy marinade, the overall flavor is not too sweet. As with many tagine or casserole dishes, the flavors improve when the dish is made a day in advance.

INGREDIENTS
2¼ lb skinless chicken thighs
1 tablespoon olive oil
1 large onion, thinly sliced
2 tablespoons light brown sugar
½ cup dry white wine
⅓ cup preserved lemons, roughly chopped
¾ cup ready-to-eat dried apricots, cut into quarters
salt and freshly ground black pepper
1 tablespoon chopped fresh cilantro
1 tablespoon chopped fresh mint
2 tablespoons slivered almonds, toasted

for the marinade:
2 teaspoons ground cumin
1 teaspoon ground coriander
½ teaspoon coarsely ground black pepper
½ teaspoon salt
3 garlic cloves, crushed
1 red chili, deseeded and finely chopped
3 tablespoons olive oil

for the couscous, to serve:
2 cups couscous
2 cups boiling water or chicken stock
2 teaspoons olive oil

1. To make the marinade, mix all the marinade ingredients in a large flat dish such as an au gratin dish. Add the chicken thighs and turn them in the marinade so that they are well coated. Cover and marinate in the refrigerator for at least 6 hours or overnight.
2. Heat the oil in the tagine base over a medium heat on the stove. Add the onion and fry gently until it is just beginning to brown. Remove from the pan.
3. Remove the chicken from the marinade and pat dry any excess liquid with kitchen paper. Add the chicken pieces to the tagine and fry until they are evenly brown.
4. Return the onion to the tagine with the sugar, wine, and preserved lemons. Stir well.
5. Cover with the tagine lid and simmer over a very low heat for 1½ hours.
6. Add the apricots, re-cover, and continue simmering for 45 minutes, checking after 35 minutes to see if the chicken is cooked through and tender.
7. When the chicken is cooked, remove the lid, and boil the sauce for a few minutes until it becomes syrupy. Adjust the seasoning to taste with some salt and pepper. Sprinkle liberally with the chopped cilantro, mint, and toasted almonds.
8. Serve with plain steamed couscous (see page 128, Steps 4 and 5).

COOKING TIPS

The recipe can also be made in a 2¼ quart braiser.

If you cook this recipe in advance, stop after Step 6 and then reheat thoroughly from Step 7, and the sauce will become syrupy.

Chickpea and Butternut Squash Tagine

SERVES: 4
PREPARATION TIME: 10 minutes
COOKING TIME: 1½ hours
COOK IN: a 2 quart tagine

INGREDIENTS
1 tablespoon olive oil
1 onion, sliced
1 butternut squash, peeled and chopped into 1½ in chunks
2 garlic cloves, minced
2oz fresh root ginger, peeled and chopped
1 tablespoon harissa paste
2 tablespoons tomato paste
1 teaspoon ground cumin
½ teaspoon turmeric
14oz can chickpeas, rinsed and drained
1 red bell pepper, deseeded and diced
¼ cup raisins
2 cups warm vegetable stock
squeeze of lime juice
salt to taste
1 tablespoon chopped fresh mint
2 tablespoons chopped fresh cilantro

for the dukka:
1 cup slivered almonds
2 tablespoons sesame seeds
1 tablespoon cumin seeds
1 tablespoon coriander seeds
1 teaspoon mixed peppercorns
¼ teaspoon salt

This recipe brings together two well-known dishes from North Africa: the tagine, a slow-cooked aromatic stew, and a dukka, which is a roasted nut and spice mixture, originating from Egypt. The content of a dukka may vary according to the cook's preferences. It is commonly served as a side dish with oil and bread, but works equally well in this recipe as a crunchy topping, adding both texture and flavor.

1. Heat the oil in the base of the tagine over a medium heat on the stove. Add the onion and squash, and fry until they begin to color and soften.

2. Add the garlic with the ginger, and cook for a further 2 minutes. Stir in the harissa paste, tomato paste, ground spices, chickpeas, red pepper, raisins, and stock. Bring to a simmer, cover with the lid, and cook over a very low heat for 1–1¼ hours.

3. To make the dukka, add the nuts, seeds, and spices to a skillet and toast for 6–8 minutes over a low to medium heat on the stove, stirring from time to time to achieve an even color and taking care not to allow the seeds to burn.

4. Grind the toasted mixture to a crumb, using either a pestle and mortar or a small blender.

5. Once the tagine has finished cooking, stir in a good squeeze of lime juice, the chopped mint, and half the cilantro, and season to taste with a little salt.

6. To serve, sprinkle the remaining cilantro over the tagine and serve the dukka in a small bowl at the table.

COOKING TIPS

The recipe can also be made in a 3½ quart braiser.

Harissa is a smooth hot paste made from chilies, tomatoes, garlic, and spices that is used in North African cuisine.

Leftover dukka can be stored in an airtight container and used as a salad topping or sprinkled on vegetables.

Fondues

Background

Fondue as it is known today originated in the mountains of Switzerland, but the name itself is derived from the French word *fondre*, meaning to "melt."

Cooking with Fondues

While countless varieties of fondue exist around the world, the most widely used recipes call for beer or white wine, starch or flour, and a mix of hard and semi-hard cheeses. Meat fondues of simmering broth or hot oil are also popular, as well as chocolate or caramel fondues with fruit or pastries for dessert.

The True Benefit of Le Creuset

Crafted from solid cast iron to retain heat longer versus ceramic fondues, Le Creuset's Traditional Fondue makes an entertaining centerpiece for special occasions and celebrations. Cast iron's versatility enables the ingredients to first be heated on the stovetop before being placed over the flame. It provides even heating and adds beauty to any dining table with its bright enamel exterior and distinctive, user-friendly design.

Cooking Tips

• It is helpful to pat meat dry before submersing it in the oil. Removing excess moisture will help prevent hot oil from splattering and causing injury.

• Avoid using olive oil—choose an oil with a high smoking point for best results.

Thai Chicken Fondue

In this light and healthy Thai variation of a fondue, chicken and vegetables are cooked in a hot broth and then noodles and greens are added at the end to make a tasty soup.

SERVES: 4
PREPARATION TIME: 20 minutes
COOKING TIME: 10 minutes, plus time cooking at the table
COOK IN: a Traditional Gourmand fondue (one size only)

INGREDIENTS

1lb boneless and skinless chicken breast
8 button mushrooms
8 scallions, cut into 2in lengths
1 small red bell pepper, deseeded and cut into strips
6oz mixed baby sweetcorn and mangetouts
2oz fine egg noodles, broken into pieces
4 cups chicken stock
1 mild red chili, thinly sliced
2 kaffir lime leaves
1 stalk lemon grass, crushed
2 slices fresh root ginger
4 Chinese leaves, shredded

for the dipping sauce:

1 mild red chili, deseeded and finely chopped
2 tablespoons light soy sauce
1 tablespoon Thai fish sauce
1 tablespoon lime juice
2 tablespoons soft brown sugar

1. To make the dipping sauce, mix all the ingredients together in a bowl. Divide among 4 dip dishes and set aside.

2. Cut the chicken into thin strips, place on 4 serving plates, and cover and chill until they are required. Divide the mushrooms, scallions, pepper, sweetcorn, and mangetouts among 4 plates, cover, and chill until required.

3. Soak the noodles in boiling water for 3–4 minutes, and then drain and transfer to a serving bowl.

4. Pour the stock into the fondue pot. Add the chili, lime leaves, lemon grass, and ginger. Bring to a boil on the stove and simmer gently for 10 minutes.

5. Transfer the fondue pot to the burner and place on the table with the prepared chicken, vegetables, noodles, and dipping sauce.

6. Using the fondue forks, cook the chicken and vegetables in the stock and then dip into the dipping sauce to eat. When this is completed, add the noodles and the Chinese leaves to the stock, reheat, and ladle the soup into bowls.

COOKING TIP

The ingredients can be varied according to taste. Raw shrimp and fish could be used instead of chicken and you can ring the changes with the vegetables too.

Traditional Cheese Fondue (Fondue Neuchâtel)

This fondue can be made with either of the traditional Swiss cheeses, Gruyère or Emmental, as both will produce an authentic consistency. Cubes of day-old French bread, with a little crust left on, are the best for dipping because they anchor well on the fondue forks. Sliced apples and broccoli florets also go well with this fondue.

SERVES: 6–8
PREPARATION TIME: 10 minutes
COOKING TIME: 10–15 minutes
COOK IN: a Traditional Gourmand fondue (one size only)

INGREDIENTS

1 garlic clove, halved
1½ cups dry white wine
4 cups coarsely grated Gruyère cheese
3 teaspoons cornstarch
2 tablespoons kirsch or vodka
a pinch of ground nutmeg
a little fresh ground black pepper
6–8oz French bread per person, cut into cubes, to serve

1. Rub the inside of the fondue pot with the cut side of the garlic. This imparts a slight flavor to the pot that will not overpower the flavor of the cheese. Discard the garlic.

2. Pour the wine into the pot and bring to a boil over a medium heat on the stove. Reduce the heat to low and gradually add the grated cheese; a small handful at a time is a good measure. Stir thoroughly to melt each handful before adding more. If too much cheese is added at once, it can become stringy or stick together in an unmanageable lump, making it difficult to melt and form the smooth consistency that you require.

3. Blend the cornstarch with the kirsch or vodka and stir into the fondue. Continue cooking and stirring until the mixture is thick and creamy. Stir in the nutmeg. Add pepper to taste.

4. Transfer the fondue pot to the stand with the lit spirit burner. Adjust the flame to a lower heat by moving the lever on the burner to close off some of the holes. A low heat will be sufficient to keep the cheese smooth and warm without sticking. Serve with the bread cubes to dip into the fondue.

COOKING TIP

Monterey Jack cheese can also be used for this fondue. If kirsch or vodka are not available, or are not liked, use a little more white wine to blend with the cornstarch.

Bitter Chocolate and Orange Fondue

If you have any chocoholics in your family or among your friends, then this fondue is a must. Fresh plump strawberries or figs go particularly well with the chocolate. This recipe is made in a small chocolate fondue, which uses a small candle to maintain the chocolate at just the right temperature.

SERVES: 6
PREPARATION TIME: 5 minutes
COOKING TIME: 10 minutes
COOK IN: a chocolate fondue

INGREDIENTS

8oz semi-sweet chocolate (minimum 70% cocoa solids), broken into pieces
finely grated zest of ½ orange
¾ cup heavy cream
1 tablespoon unsalted butter
2 tablespoons Cointreau or other orange-flavored liqueur
fruit, to serve

1. Put the chocolate into the fondue pot and melt over a low heat on the stove. Add the orange zest, cream, and butter as the chocolate begins to melt. Keep stirring until all the ingredients are melted. Stir in the Cointreau.

2. Transfer the fondue pot to its stand above the lit candle flame to keep it warm. Stir occasionally, if you are not serving immediately. Serve with fruit to dip into the fondue.

COOKING TIPS

A larger traditional Gourmande fondue set can also be used for this recipe, but remember to keep the burner flame very low to avoid burning the chocolate.

Allow approximately 2oz of dipping ingredients per person.

For a special occasion, stir in 2 tablespoons of your favorite liqueur to the melted chocolate mixture. If you are serving this fondue to children, then use orange juice instead of liqueur.

Terrines

Background

Long appreciated as both a cooking and serving dish, the Pâté Terrine is drawn from early Le Creuset designs of the 1930s and 1940s, and today it is used for a wide variety of recipes like foie gras, bread, cake, custard, and hard cheese.

Cooking with Terrines

Terrine dishes are traditionally used to compact a forcemeat mixture like pâté (the resulting form is also referred to as a terrine). Some terrines include a weighted press that molds the mixture from all sides. As the meat cools, the fat within it begins to set, helping the terrine hold its form.

The True Benefit of Le Creuset

The enameled cast iron Pâté Terrine makes a stylish serving pan for meatloaf, fresh bread, pound cake, or homemade custard—and its temperature retention properties allow the dish to remain hot or cold at the table until food is ready to serve. The small hole in the lid allows a small amount of steam to escape when necessary, keeping the dish's contents balanced and preventing them from becoming too moist.

Cooking Tips

• When preparing very soft or light cake mixtures, lining the terrine dish with a strip of parchment paper will make turning out easier. Simply allow the dish to cool before turning out for best results.

• When preparing uncooked pâtés, lining the dish is not necessary unless the contents must be turned out whole.

Meatloaf with Oven-Roasted Tomatoes

SERVES: 8
PREPARATION TIME: 15 minutes
COOKING TIME: 1 hour 20 minutes
COOK IN: a 1½ quart pâté terrine

A classic meatloaf is quick and easy to prepare, and is equally delicious served hot with roasted tomatoes or cold with pickles and salad. The Le Creuset terrine is a perfect shape for baking it in and the lid protects it from drying out.

INGREDIENTS

1 tablespoon oil
1 tablespoon butter
1 large onion, finely chopped
2 garlic cloves, crushed
1½ lb lean ground beef
10½ oz ground pork
1 green bell pepper, deseeded and finely chopped
2 eggs, beaten
1 cup fresh breadcrumbs
1 teaspoon mixed dried herbs
3 tablespoons chopped fresh parsley
2 tablespoons finely chopped gherkins
1 tablespoon Worcestershire sauce
1 tablespoon tomato ketchup
2 teaspoons salt
freshly ground black pepper

for the roasted tomatoes:

16 small vine tomatoes (not cherry)
2 garlic cloves, thinly sliced
salt and freshly ground black pepper
2 tablespoons olive oil

1. Preheat the oven to 350°F. Heat the oil and butter in a small frying pan, add the onion and garlic, and cook gently until soft. Leave to cool.

2. In a large bowl, use your hands to mix together the meat, bell pepper, eggs, breadcrumbs, dried herbs, fresh parsley, gherkins, Worcestershire sauce, ketchup, cooled onion and garlic mixture, and salt and pepper.

3. Line the base of the terrine with a strip of parchment paper.

4. Press the mixture into the terrine. Cover with the lid and cook in the oven for 45 minutes. Remove the lid and bake for a further 15 minutes.

5. About 5 minutes before the end of the cooking time, halve the tomatoes and place them, cut side facing upward, in a roasting or au gratin dish. Scatter over the garlic, season with salt and pepper, and drizzle over the olive oil. Roast in the oven for 20 minutes.

6. Remove the meatloaf from the oven and leave to stand while the tomatoes are cooking. It will keep hot in the terrine and allowing it to stand makes it easier to slice.

7. Before turning out the meatloaf, run a round-ended knife around the edges of the terrine to release it. Remove the strip of parchment paper before slicing and serving with the tomatoes.

COOKING TIP

If you are planning to serve the meatloaf cold, place a weight on it while it is still warm. This makes it easy to slice neatly.

Coarse Country Pâté

This pâté has bold peppery flavors and a firm coarse texture. The outer wrapping of bacon and bay leaves is not difficult to do and makes the finished dish so attractive for a lunch or buffet table.

MAKES: 12–14 slices
PREPARATION TIME: 30 minutes
COOKING TIME: 2–2½ hours
COOK IN: a 1½ quart pâté terrine

INGREDIENTS
8oz bacon
4 bay leaves
12oz lean ground pork
8oz boneless chicken thigh meat, finely chopped
8oz chicken livers, chopped
2 shallots, finely chopped
2 garlic cloves, crushed
1 tablespoon mixed whole peppercorns
1 tablespoon chopped fresh thyme
1 tablespoon chopped fresh sage
1 teaspoon salt
¼ teaspoon freshly ground black pepper
3 large eggs
3 tablespoons brandy

1. Thin the bacon by pressing it out on a board with a round-bladed knife. Lay the 4 bay leaves along the bottom of the terrine and then line the bottom and sides with the bacon slices positioned side by side. Leave a little of the bacon overhanging the sides of the dish. Reserve any extra bacon.

2. Preheat the oven to 300°F. Put the pork, chicken, and chicken livers into a bowl with all the other ingredients. Stir together thoroughly. Transfer the mixture to the lined dish, leveling the top. Use the overhanging pieces of bacon and any reserved bacon to enclose the pâté.

3. Put on the lid and stand the terrine in a bain-marie. To do this, place the covered terrine inside a much larger dish containing water. The water level should reach about halfway up the side walls of the terrine and be topped up with hot water if necessary.

4. Bake the pâté in the oven for 2–2½ hours or until the juices in the center of the pâté run clear when pierced with a skewer or toothpick. Remove the terrine from the bain-marie and set aside to cool completely before unmolding. Leave the lid on as the pâté cools. Unmold onto a large serving dish, trimming away any meat solids that have escaped. Cut into even slices with a very sharp knife.

COOKING TIPS

The recipe can also be made in a 2 quart French oven.

A bain-marie is often used for pâtés and terrines because it allows the mixture to cook very gently without coloring or baking, resulting in an even texture throughout.

Turkey meat can be used instead of chicken.

This recipe freezes well for up to 1 month. Thaw completely before use.

A red Burgundy or Oregon Pinot Noir makes a good partner for the pâté and can stand up to its assertive flavor.

Onion and Olive Bread

The smell of freshly baked bread is hard to beat, but the thought of making it can be daunting. However, there is no need to feel that way because with a single-mixing-and-rising recipe such as this, no previous bread-making experience is necessary.

MAKES: 12 slices
PREPARATION TIME: 20 minutes, plus 1–1½ hours rising time
COOKING TIME: 35–40 minutes
COOK IN: a 1½ quart (32cm) pâté terrine

INGREDIENTS

- 6 cups white bread flour, plus extra for dusting
- 1 medium onion, finely chopped
- 3 tablespoons olive oil, plus extra for greasing
- 1 teaspoon salt
- ½ teaspoon freshly ground black pepper
- ¼ oz envelope of active-dry yeast
- ½ cup milk
- ½ cup pitted black olives, roughly chopped
- 1 teaspoon coarse sea salt

1. Grease and flour the inside of the pâté terrine. The lid is not used for this recipe.
2. Put the onion and 1 tablespoon of the oil into a microwave bowl, cover, and microwave on full power for 1½–2 minutes until the onion is soft. Set aside to cool.
3. Sift the flour and salt into a large bowl and stir in the pepper and yeast.
4. Put 1½ cups of very hot water into a bowl and add the cold milk to give the correct temperature for mixing. Add the remaining oil as well.
5. Stir the onions and olives into the dry ingredients, then gradually stir in the liquid. The dough should be slightly wet, but not sticky; if it seems too dry, add a little more milk. Turn out the dough onto a well-floured surface and knead for 1–2 minutes. Form it into a long roll about the length of the terrine.
6. Transfer the dough to the dish with any seams or folds tucked underneath. Make a few slashes across the top of the dough. Brush the top with a little olive oil. Cover loosely with plastic wrap and leave for 1–1½ hours in a warm place to rise until the dough is just above the rim. Sprinkle with the sea salt just before baking. Preheat the oven to 375°F.
7. Bake the bread in the center of the oven for 35–40 minutes until risen and golden brown. Leave to cool in the dish for 10 minutes before unmolding onto a wire rack to cool completely.

COOKING TIPS

You can replace the olives with ½ cup of sun-dried tomatoes for a change of flavor.

If you like a really soft crust, cover the freshly baked warm bread with a clean dish-towel while it cools.

Lemon Pound Cake

This recipe holds true to the pound cake rules of using equal quantities of the main ingredients—namely, butter, sugar, flour, and eggs. Cooking this light, moist, lemony cake in the terrine also makes it easy to cut and share.

PREPARATION TIME: 20 minutes
COOKING TIME: 35–40 minutes
COOK IN: a 1½ quart pâté terrine

INGREDIENTS

zest and juice of 2 large lemons
4 tablespoons strained plain yogurt
2 teaspoons vanilla extract
a few drops of yellow food coloring (optional)
8oz softened butter, plus a little extra for greasing
8oz superfine sugar
4 extra large eggs
8oz self-rising flour, sifted
1 teaspoon baking powder

for the lemon icing:
zest and juice of ½ large lemon
8 heaped tablespoons powdered sugar
lemon zest, to decorate

1. Prepare the terrine by greasing with a little softened butter and lining the base with a strip of parchment paper. Preheat the oven to 350°F.
2. In a small bowl, mix together the lemon zest, lemon juice, yogurt, vanilla extract, and food coloring (if using). Set aside.
3. In a larger bowl, cream together the butter and the sugar until light and fluffy. Beat in the eggs one at a time.
4. Fold in the sifted flour and baking powder, followed by the lemon and yogurt mixture.
5. Pour the mixture into the prepared terrine and smooth over the top with a spatula.
6. Bake in the center of the oven for 35–40 minutes until the top is golden and firm to the touch. When the cake is done, a skewer or toothpick inserted into the center will come out clean. After baking, leave the cake to cool in the terrine for at least 15 minutes before turning it out onto a wire rack.
7. To make the lemon icing, beat together the lemon juice, lemon zest, and powdered sugar until smooth.
8. Pour the icing over the slightly warm cake and allow to set. Decorate with lemon zest.
9. Cool thoroughly before storing the cake in the cleaned dish or an airtight container.

Tatins

Background

Legend has it that the beloved dessert, tarte Tatin, originated in the kitchen of the Tatin sisters, who operated a hotel in the French town of Lamotte-Beuvron. While making a pie for guests, one sister mistakenly placed the prepared apples in the dish first. She decided to lay the pastry crust on top, and turn it out after it had finished baking. The result was unsual, but delicious, and it became the signature dish of Hotel Tatin.

Cooking with Tatin Dishes

Named for this famous French upside-down apple tarte, the enameled cast iron Tarte Tatin is a capable alternative for a variety of recipes like pizza and quiche when used in place of a conventional pie dish.

The True Benefit of Le Creuset

The inverted handles on this unique dish are designed to delicately turn out upside-down cakes, fruit pies, and the classic French pastry that shares its name.

Cooking Tips

• It is recommended to grease the tatin dish when baking a cake; however, when making pastry tatins, greasing is unnecessary. Simply line the dish with the pastry and add the sweet or savory filling of your choice.

• When turning out a finished tatin, tap the dish a few times with a wooden spoon before removing it to ensure clean separation of the contents.

Caramelized Tomato Tarte Tatin with Goat Cheese

This light and fresh-tasting tart is best made in the summer when tomatoes are at their most flavorsome. It makes an ideal lunch or light meal served with a crisp dressed salad.

SERVES: 6
PREPARATION TIME: 15 minutes
COOKING TIME: 50 minutes
COOK IN: a 2 quart tatin

INGREDIENTS
flour, for dusting
8oz ready-made puff pastry pie crust
2oz goat cheese (broken into small pieces), to serve

for the onion layer:
2 tablespoons olive oil
1 tablespoon butter
2 large onions, sliced
2 garlic cloves, minced
1 tablespoon brown sugar
¼ teaspoon salt
½ teaspoon black pepper

for the caramelized tomatoes:
1 tablespoon brown sugar
3–4 tablespoons water
1 tablespoon white balsamic vinegar
1 tablespoon butter
pinch of salt
1lb medium-sized vine tomatoes, cut in half
leaves from 2–3 fresh thyme sprigs

1. Preheat the oven to 400°F. To prepare the onion layer, heat the oil and butter in the dish on the stove over a low to medium heat. Once the butter has melted, add the onions, garlic, sugar, and seasoning. Cook, stirring occasionally, until golden brown and caramelized. Empty the contents into a bowl, set to one side, and clean the dish.

2. To prepare the tomatoes, put the brown sugar and water in the clean tatin and set on the stove over a low to medium heat.

3. Once the mixture begins to caramelize, remove from the heat, allowing the cast iron's heat-retentive properties to finish the process. Stir in the balsamic vinegar, butter, and salt, taking care as the mixture may splatter a little. Pack the tomatoes, cut side facing down, into the dish and sprinkle with the fresh thyme leaves.

4. Spoon the cooked onion mixture over the tomatoes.

5. On a lightly floured surface, roll out the pie-crust dough so that it is 1¼ –1½in larger than the top of the dish. Place the pie-crust sheet over the tomatoes and onions, tucking the edges down around the outside. This will form a rim to contain the filling when it's turned out. Make 3–4 steam holes in the pie crust before placing in the oven for 25–30 minutes. The crust should be well risen and golden brown when done.

6. Leave for a couple of minutes before loosening around the edge with a round-bladed knife. Invert onto a wide shallow plate with a rim. Scatter the goat cheese over the top of the tarte and serve immediately.

COOKING TIP

Other full-flavored cheeses such as manchego, white Stilton, or Taleggio also work well.

Caramelized Shallot Tarte Tatin

Shallots have a mild, sweet flavor and taste wonderful once caramelized in this quick, simple, and easy recipe. Enjoy this tarte tatin as a mouth-watering light supper with a fresh salad or some seasonal vegetables.

SERVES: 6
PREPARATION TIME: 20 minutes
COOKING TIME: 1 hour
COOK IN: a 2 quart tatin

INGREDIENTS
1½ lb shallots
½ stick butter
3 tablespoons balsamic vinegar
2 tablespoons superfine sugar
1 cup chicken stock
1 teaspoon fresh thyme leaves
salt and freshly ground black pepper
1 pack ready-rolled puff pastry

1. Peel the shallots. Some will split in two, but you will need to cut the remainder in half lengthwise. Heat a tatin on the stove. Melt the butter in the dish and add the shallots. Cook over a medium heat until they start to brown.

2. Add the balsamic vinegar, sugar, and chicken stock. Continue cooking until the shallots are soft and the liquid has reduced and become sticky and caramelized. This can take up to 30 minutes. Scatter over the thyme leaves and season with salt and pepper.

3. Heat the oven to 400°F. Cut a circle from the pastry, a little bigger than the tatin, lay it over the shallots, and tuck down the sides. Cook in the oven for 20–25 minutes until the pastry is puffed and golden.

4. Leave the tart to stand in the dish for 2 minutes. Run a round-ended knife around the edge of the pastry before turning it out onto a flat plate to serve.

COOKING TIPS

The recipe can also be made in a 1¾ quart skillet or a 2¼ quart braiser.

Shallots look particularly attractive in this tarte tatin, but, as an alternative, you could also use halved or quartered mild sweet onions such as Vidalia.

Apple Tarte Tatin

This famous recipe arose by accident at the Hotel Tatin in the French town of Lamotte-Beuvron. The Tatin sisters, Caroline and Stephanie, had inherited the hotel in 1888. Stephanie's cooking had a good reputation but, one day, she put a pastry crust over some apples instead of putting the apples in a pastry shell. To make the result appear the same as her usual apple tart, Stephanie turned it upside down. Her diners loved it. In the oven, the apples, sugar, and butter had intensified their caramel flavor and the pastry was dry, light, and crisp. A Le Creuset tatin, with cleverly designed handles for easy "turn over," is ideal for this recipe.

SERVES: 6–8
PREPARATION TIME: 15 minutes
COOKING TIME: 30 minutes
COOK IN: a 2 quart tatin

INGREDIENTS
5 large dessert apples (such as Golden Delicious or Granny Smith)
⅓ cup white sugar
⅓ cup butter
2 tablespoons lemon juice
8oz store-bought puff pastry
whipped cream or ice cream, to serve

1. Peel, quarter, and core the apples. Cover them with cold water to stop discoloration.

2. Preheat the oven to 400°F. Put the sugar and butter into the tatin and melt the butter over a medium heat on the stove, stirring to dissolve the sugar evenly. Cook for a few minutes until the sugar and butter begin to caramelize and turn a light golden brown. Remove from the heat.

3. Drain the apples well and then place them, rounded side facing down, to tightly fill the pan's bottom. Sprinkle with the lemon juice.

4. Leave to cool for a few minutes while rolling out the dough. Roll the dough into a circle that is the same size as the top of the dish. Place it lightly over the apples, tucking the edges down around the fruit so that it forms a rim to contain the filling when it is turned out. Make 4 small steam holes.

5. Transfer to the oven and bake on the top shelf for 15–20 minutes until the crust is well risen and golden brown.

6. Leave the tart to rest for 5 minutes before loosening around the edge with a round-bladed knife. Invert onto a wide shallow plate with a rim to catch any caramel before serving warm with the whipped cream or ice cream.

COOKING TIPS

The recipe can also be made in a 1¾ quart skillet or a 2¼ quart braiser.

Plums, peaches, nectarines, or apricots can be used instead of apples.

Maple Pecan Pie

A tatin is an extremely versatile piece of cooking equipment. It is ideal for baking pastry tarts, quiches, and pies because there is no need to blind-bake the pastry first before adding the filling.

SERVES: 8–10
PREPARATION TIME: 25 minutes, plus 1½ hours chilling time
COOKING TIME: 1 hour
COOK IN: a 2 quart tatin

INGREDIENTS

for the pie crust:

2 cups all-purpose flour, plus extra for dusting
1 stick butter
1 tablespoon powdered sugar
1 large egg yolk

for the filling:

6 large eggs
¾ cup soft brown sugar
1 cup maple syrup
¾ cup corn syrup
1 stick butter, melted
1 teaspoon vanilla extract
3 cups pecans, coarsely chopped
whipped cream or ice cream, to serve

1. To make the pie crust, sift the flour into a bowl. Rub in the butter until the mixture resembles fine breadcrumbs. Stir in the powdered sugar. With a knife, stir in the egg yolk and 1 tablespoon of water until the mixture forms a dough. Knead lightly into a ball, wrap in plastic wrap, and then chill for 1 hour.

2. On a lightly floured surface, roll out the pastry to fit the tatin dish. Lift the pastry into the dish and press onto the bottom and up the sides of the pan. Trim off any excess pie crust. Chill for 30 minutes.

3. Preheat the oven to 325°F. In a bowl, whisk together the eggs and brown sugar until well blended. Whisk in the maple syrup, corn syrup, melted butter, and vanilla extract. Stir in the pecans. Pour the mixture into the pie-crust case. Bake in the oven for 50 minutes to 1 hour until the filling has set. If the tart is browning too quickly, cover with aluminum foil.

4. Leave to cool slightly before serving with whipped cream or ice cream. This tart is best served at room temperature.

COOKING TIPS

The recipe can also be made in a 1¾ quart skillet or a 2¼ quart brasier.

If time is short, use ready-made, sweet pie crust. Look for a good-quality brand which is made from butter for the best results.

Doufeus

Background

In the 1600s, cast iron Dutch ovens were designed to be placed directly onto a heat source such as burning wood or embers. Cooks would pile coal or embers on top of the vessel in order to surround the food with heat, thus creating an oven effect. Originally introduced in 1934, the Le Creuset Doufeu features a recessed lid designed to hold ice rather than embers, as an aid for slow cooking.

Cooking with Doufeus

The Doufeu can be used just like any round or oval oven, but it has added performance benefits when it comes to slow cooking. As moisture begins to evaporate inside, the ice-filled lid causes this moisture to condense. Specially designed dimples on the flat interior of the lid then direct the moisture back down onto the food.

The True Benefit of Le Creuset

The self-basting effect of Le Creuset's classic Doufeu minimizes the need to add additional water and ensures that food remains moist, nutrients are not lost and flavors intensify.

Cooking Tips

• Even when the ice in the Doufeu lid melts, the self-basting process continues to function, as long as water in the lid remains below the boiling point.

• The Doufeu method of cooking is especially helpful for tenderizing cuts of meat or poultry, using moist, gentle heat to soften tough fibers. This versatile design is also useful for preparing stews, roasted meats, soup and rice dishes.

Beef Bourguignon

SERVES: 8
PREPARATION TIME: 20 minutes
COOKING TIME: 2½–3 hours
COOK IN: a 7¼ quart oval doufeu

INGREDIENTS
3–4 tablespoons olive oil
10oz smoked bacon lardons
3lb 5oz lean chuck steak, cut into large chunks
3 cups full-bodied red wine, at room temperature
3 garlic cloves, finely minced
2 tablespoons tomato paste
1 cup hot double-strength beef stock
2 medium carrots, thinly sliced
1 bouquet garni (made up of a few fresh parsley, thyme, and rosemary sprigs and 2 fresh bay leaves)
salt and freshly ground black pepper
3 tablespoons chopped fresh parsley, to serve

for the caramelized shallots and mushrooms:
4 tablespoons butter
14oz small shallots or white pickling onions
14oz small button mushrooms

for the beurre manié to thicken:
3 tablespoons softened butter
2 tablespoons all-purpose flour

Beef Bourguignon is a casserole that delivers on all levels with an intensely flavored red wine sauce and beef that melts in the mouth. The large capacity of a doufeu means that it is perfect for making the large portions needed for a family gathering or party. Serve with creamy mash potatoes, lightly steamed green vegetables, and some real French bread.

1. Heat 3 tablespoons of the olive oil in the doufeu over a medium heat. Add the bacon lardons and cook until lightly browned. Remove with a slotted spoon onto a plate (retaining the oil in the doufeu) and set to one side.

2. Fry the meat in 2–3 batches, adding small amounts at a time and removing from the doufeu once lightly browned. Add a little more olive oil between batches if necessary.

3. Return the bacon lardons and the removed beef to the doufeu. Add the wine a third at a time, stirring well to release any caramelized juices from the base of the doufeu.

4. Stir in the garlic, tomato paste, beef stock, carrots, the bouquet garni, and 2 teaspoons of black pepper. Bring the contents to a simmer over a medium heat. Once simmering, reduce the heat to low, put on the lid, and fill with ice or ice-cold water. Cook for 2 hours, topping up the water as necessary.

5. Half an hour before the beef finishes cooking, caramelize the shallots and mushrooms by melting 2 tablespoons of the butter in a skillet over a low to medium heat. Add the shallots and fry for 10–15 minutes until golden brown and caramelized. This requires patience as slow caramelization will produce a deeper flavor. Transfer to a plate with a slotted spoon.

6. Melt the remaining 2 tablespoons of butter in the skillet, add the mushrooms, and gently fry until nicely browned.

7. After the 2 hours cooking time is over, carefully remove the lid from the doufeu and discard any remaining water. Remove the bouquet garni.

8. For the beurre manié, blend the butter and flour in a small bowl. Add to the doufeu in small amounts, stirring after each addition until it has all been incorporated. Stir in the caramelized shallots and mushrooms. Simmer for 10–15 minutes to reduce and thicken.

9. Stir well, adjust the seasoning to taste, and sprinkle with the parsley before serving.

LE CREUSET

Coq Au Vin

SERVES: 8–10
PREPARATION TIME: 25 minutes
COOKING TIME: about 3 hours
COOK IN: a 7¼ quart oval doufeu

There are many versions of this classic French dish, most cooked in a full-bodied red wine. However, the main ingredient is always a cockerel. Unfortunately, few of us have access to these full-flavored birds, so always use a good-quality chicken instead.

INGREDIENTS

2 tablespoons extra-virgin olive oil
2 cups chopped bacon
1 medium onion, chopped
2 x 4½ lb chickens, each cut into 8 pieces
5 tablespoons brandy
1 bouquet garni (made up of a few fresh parsley, thyme, and rosemary sprigs and 2 fresh bay leaves)
3 garlic cloves, crushed
1 tablespoon tomato paste
1 tablespoon lemon juice
1 tablespoon sugar
3 cups full-bodied, dry red wine (such as a Burgundy or Pinot Noir)
2 tablespoons chopped fresh flat-leaf parsley, to garnish

for the glazed shallots and mushrooms:

2 tablespoons butter
1 tablespoon olive oil
12oz shallots
12oz button mushrooms

for the beurre manié to thicken:

2 tablespoons butter, softened
3 tablespoons all-purpose flour

1. Heat the oil in the doufeu over a medium heat on the stove. Add the bacon and onion, and cook, stirring, until both are softened. Remove and drain well.

2. Fry the chicken in batches until all of the pieces are evenly browned, and then return them to the doufeu with the bacon and onion. Remove the doufeu from the heat and add the brandy. Carefully ignite, standing well back until the flames subside, and then return the doufeu to the heat.

3. Put the bouquet garni into the doufeu with the garlic, tomato paste, lemon juice, sugar, and red wine. Cover with the lid and fill the recess with ice or ice-cold water. Cook on the stove over a low heat for 2 hours until the chicken is very tender.

4. About 30 minutes before the chicken finishes cooking, make the glazed shallots and mushrooms by melting the butter and oil in a frying pan over a medium heat. Add the shallots and fry for 10–15 minutes until golden brown and soft. Transfer to a plate. Add the mushrooms to the pan and toss so that they are just cooked and colored.

5. Carefully lift the lid of the doufeu and discard the remaining water. Lift out the cooked chicken pieces onto the warm upturned lid or a plate. Skim away any unwanted oil from the doufeu and discard the herb bundle.

6. To make the beurre manié, blend the butter and flour together in a small bowl. Add to the doufeu in small amounts, stirring after each addition so that the sauce remains smooth. When all the beurre manié has been incorporated, simmer for 8–10 minutes to reduce the sauce to a light coating consistency.

7. Return the chicken, shallots, and mushrooms to the doufeu. Simmer for a few minutes until all the contents are piping hot. Sprinkle generously with the parsley and serve.

COOKING TIP

You should not need to add any extra ice or water to the doufeu during cooking.

Cranberry and Mustard Glazed Ham

A succulent ham joint is slowly cooked in a spiced vegetable and fruit broth, coated in a sweet cranberry and mustard glaze, and then roasted until deep golden brown. This is a dish that can be served hot or cold all year round. It is also ideal for special-occasion meals.

SERVES: 8
PREPARATION TIME: 15–20 minutes
COOKING TIME: 3¼–3¾ hours
COOK IN: a 7¼ quart oval doufeu

INGREDIENTS

4½–5½ lb boned gammon or raw ham joint
2 onions, quartered
2 carrots, chopped
2 celery sticks, chopped
2 eating apples, peeled, cored, and quartered
½ teaspoon cloves
1 teaspoon juniper berries
a handful of fresh parsley
3 bay leaves
2 cups dry cider or unsweetened pressed apple juice

for the glaze:

3 tablespoons ready-made cranberry preserve or sauce
3 tablespoons light muscovado sugar
2 teaspoons wholegrain mustard

1. Place the joint in the doufeu, cover with water, and bring to a boil over a medium heat. Once simmering, turn off the heat and allow to cool slightly. Remove the joint and discard the liquid from the pan at this stage.

2. Return the joint to the pan and add the vegetables, apples, spices, herbs, and cider or apple juice.

3. Add enough water to the contents of the pan to cover the joint by three-quarters, and bring to a simmer.

4. Put on the lid and fill with ice or ice-cold water. Reduce the heat to low. Cook for 2¾–3 hours. Replenish the ice or water, as required.

5. Preheat the oven to 375°F. Allow the ham to cool slightly before removing it from the stock into a roasting dish.

6. Remove the top layer of skin, leaving the fat layer. Using a knife, score the fat with diagonal strokes, 1in apart, in both directions in order to create a diamond pattern.

7. Mix together the glaze ingredients and apply liberally to the scored ham fat using a silicone basting brush.

8. Place in the hot oven and cook for 20–25 minutes until the top of the ham is glossy and caramelized around the edges.

9. Allow to cool slightly before carving. Serve generously sliced hot or cold.

French-Style Braised Lamb with Beans and Red Wine

In this delicious dish, the steamy atmosphere created by the stock and wine in the doufeu produces very juicy and tender meat. The beans and vegetables make this a robust and rustic meal for a cold winter's day.

SERVES: 6–8
PREPARATION TIME: 15 minutes
COOKING TIME: 3 hours
COOK IN: a 7¼ quart doufeu

INGREDIENTS
4–4½ lb leg of lamb
2 garlic cloves, cut into quarters
8 rosemary sprigs, broken into small pieces
12 shallots, peeled and left whole
6 medium-sized carrots, cut into chunks
2 celery sticks, cut into chunks
2 bay leaves
2 cups red wine
1 cup double-strength lamb stock
14oz can flageolet or cannellini beans, rinsed and drained
2 teaspoons redcurrant jelly
1–1½ tablespoons cornstarch, mixed with a little water to make a paste
salt and freshly ground black pepper

1. Trim the lamb of any excess pieces of fat. Pierce the flesh several times and push the pieces of garlic and rosemary into the holes.
2. Put the lamb into the doufeu, and season well with some salt and pepper. Place all the prepared vegetables around the meat with any remaining rosemary sprigs and the bay leaves. Pour over the wine and stock.
3. Place the doufeu on the stovetop and bring the contents to a simmer over a medium heat. Once simmering, reduce the heat to low, put on the lid, and fill with ice or ice-cold water. Cook the lamb for 2¾–3 hours or until it is very tender. Top up the water as necessary.
4. Carefully remove the lid and discard any water. Transfer the lamb to a warm serving platter, cover with aluminum foil, and leave to rest.
5. Skim away any excess oil from the stock and remove the rosemary sprigs and bay leaves. Stir in the beans and simmer without the lid to reduce the stock by about one third.
6. Stir in the redcurrant jelly and enough of the cornstarch and water mixture for the sauce to become thick and glossy. Season to taste.
7. Serve the meat, cut thickly, with the vegetable and bean sauce.

COOKING TIPS

The carved meat can be returned to the doufeu with the sauce and the lid replaced to keep warm ready for serving.

You'll find that Potato Dauphinoise goes particularly well with this dish. For the recipe, turn to page 98.

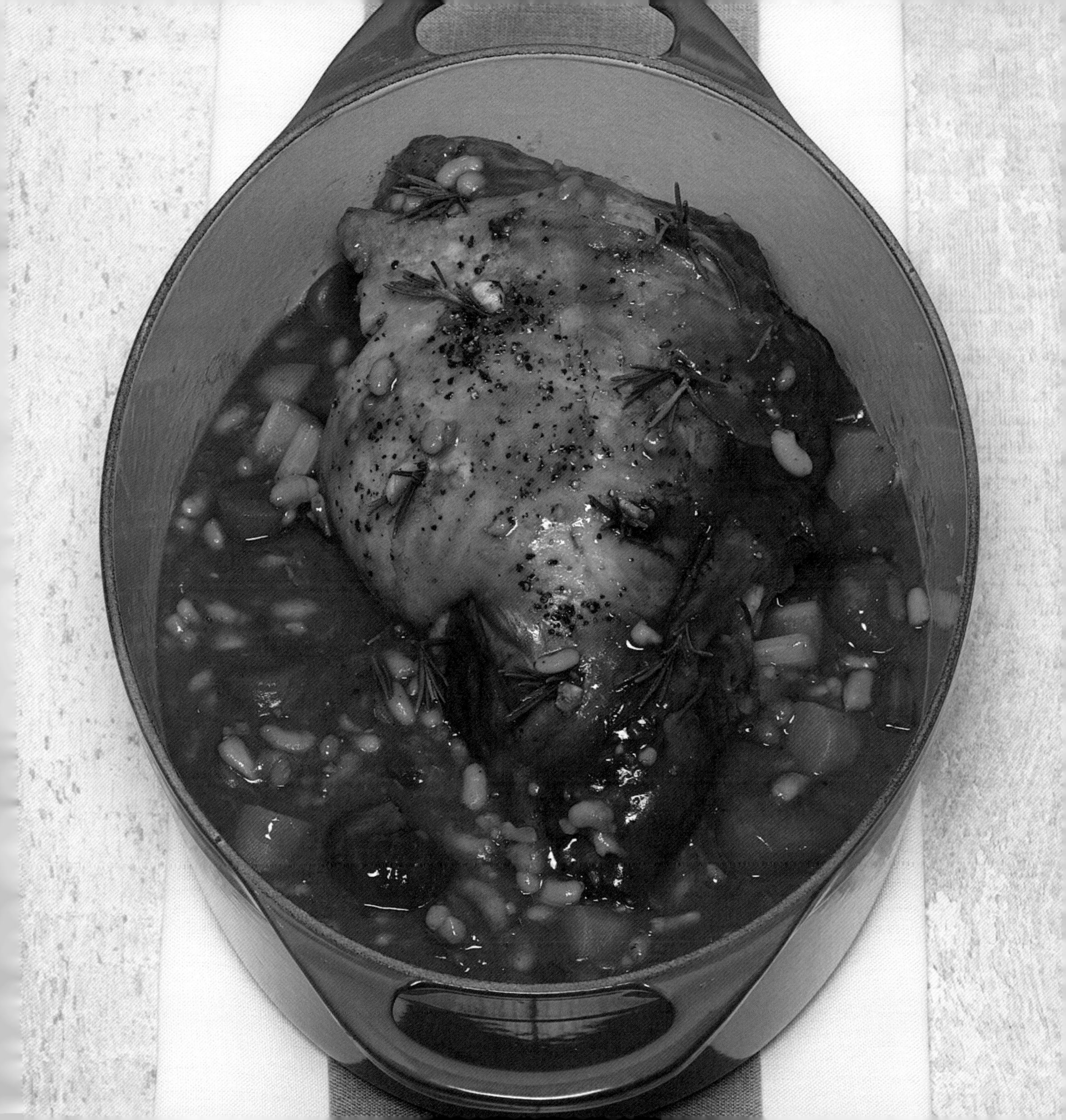

Index